150 World Cuisine Recipes

(150 World Cuisine Recipes - Volume 1)

Penny Cook

Copyright: Published in the United States by Penny Cook/ © PENNY COOK

Published on November, 19 2020

All rights reserved. No part of this publication may be reproduced, stored in retrieval system, copied in any form or by any means, electronic, mechanical, photocopying, recording or otherwise transmitted without written permission from the publisher. Please do not participate in or encourage piracy of this material in any way. You must not circulate this book in any format. PENNY COOK does not control or direct users' actions and is not responsible for the information or content shared, harm and/or actions of the book readers.

In accordance with the U.S. Copyright Act of 1976, the scanning, uploading and electronic sharing of any part of this book without the permission of the publisher constitute unlawful piracy and theft of the author's intellectual property. If you would like to use material from the book (other than just simply for reviewing the book), prior permission must be obtained by contacting the author at author@shrimpcookbook.com

Thank you for your support of the author's rights.

Content

CHAPTER 1: ASIAN RECIPES 5

1. Asian Chicken, Vegetable And Almond Stir Fry 5
2. Asian Pork & Vegetable Stir Fry For Two . 5
3. Asparagus Beef Ramen Bowl 6
4. Better Than Takeout Moo Shu Pork 6
5. Bibimbap (Korean Mixed Rice) 7
6. Easy Chicken Skewers With Peanut Sauce . 7
7. Easy Chicken Teriyaki Recipe 8
8. General Tso Chicken 8
9. Grilled Teriyaki Chicken With Ramen Noodles 9
10. Indian Style Sunehari Salmon 10
11. Japanese Cucumber Salad 10
12. Japanese Pancakes 11
13. Matcha Shortbread Cookies 11
14. Matcha Truffles 12
15. Omurice (Japanese Stir Fried Rice With Eggs) 12
16. Simple Thai Peanut Pork 13
17. Sizzling Vegetable Salad 13
18. Spicy Chicken Yaki Soba Noodle Salad 14
19. Teriyaki Pork Ramen Stir Fry 15
20. Teriyaki Steak Skewers 15
21. Teriyaki Glazed Water Chestnuts With Bacon 16
22. Thai Chicken With Sugar Snap Peas 16
23. Thai Coffee 17
24. Thai Curried Tilapia Skillet 17
25. Thai Curry Chicken & Rice 18
26. Thai Drunken Noodles 18
27. Thai Noodle Salad 19
28. Thai Peanut Chicken 19
29. Thai BBQ Slow Cooker Ribs 20

CHAPTER 2: CHINESE RECIPES 20

30. Asian Beef Ribs 20
31. Asian Meatballs With Lo Mein Noodles ... 21
32. Asian Peanut Noodles With Beef For Two 21
33. Baked Shrimp Rangoon Appetizers 22
34. Bok Choy Stir Fry With Shrimp 22
35. Chicken Lo Mein 23

36. Chicken Cabbage Noodle Salad 23
37. Chinese Orange Chicken Recipe 24
38. Chinese Shrimp Recipe 24
39. Chinese Takeout Style Lemon Chicken 25
40. Chinese Style Pork Stir Fry 25
41. Coconut Almond Cookies 26
42. Crispy Wontons With Asian Dipping Sauce 26
43. Crunchy Asian Salad 27
44. Easy Chicken Stir Fry 27
45. Easy Chinese Stir Fry 28
46. Fresh Pineapple Tapioca 28
47. Orange Ginger Beef Stir Fry 29
48. Shrimp Fried Rice Recipe 29
49. Sizzling Shrimp Stir Fry 30
50. Speedy Ginger Chicken Soup Bowls 30
51. Szechuan Beef Stir Fry 31
52. Tofu Stir Fry Recipe 31
53. Wonton Soup 32

CHAPTER 3: INDIAN RECIPES 32

54. Aloo Matar 32
55. Baked Butter Chicken 33
56. Chicken Biryani Recipe 33
57. Chickpea And Tomato Stew 34
58. Creamy Chicken Korma 34
59. Creamy Indian Butter Chicken 35
60. Creamy Indian Chutney Dip 35
61. Curried Chicken And Rice 36
62. Easy Coconut Curry 36
63. India Inspired Chocolate Coconut Burfi ... 37
64. Indian Chicken Curry 37
65. Indian Chicken Curry Recipe 38
66. Indian Chicken Tikka Masala 38
67. Indian Peanut Butter Nankhatai Cookies .. 39
68. Indian Vegetarian Dal Biryani 40
69. Indian Style Chicken Koftas 40
70. Indian Style Grilled Chicken Tikka 41
71. Indian Style Sheer Khurma Dessert 41
72. Indian Style Stir Fried Tandoori Shrimp ... 42
73. Madras Curry Chicken 42
74. Mango Chutney Curry Dip 43
75. One Pot Curry & Rice 43
76. Sri Lankan Fish Curry 44
77. Tandoori Chicken 44

CHAPTER 4: SOUTHERN RECIPES 45

78. Baking Powder Biscuits 45
79. Bananas Foster Cheesecake Squares ... 45
80. Blackened Tilapia Po' Boy 46
81. Buttermilk Biscuits 46
82. Carolina Style BBQ Pulled Pork Sliders 47
83. Chicken 'n Waffle Tacos 47
84. Cookie Crumb Topped Apple Crisp 48
85. Family Reunion Macaroni Salad 48
86. Iyanla's Divine Mac & Cheese 49
87. Mac And Cheese Jalapeño Bites 49
88. Memphis Style Muffuletta 50
89. Mini Memphis Style BBQ Burgers 50
90. Oven Fried Catfish Recipe 51
91. Peach Cobbler Recipe 51
92. Praline Sweet Potatoes 52
93. Red Beans & Rice Soul Food Recipe 52
94. Simple Southern Style 'Unfried' Chicken .. 53
95. Slow Cooker Black Eyed Peas 53
96. Sour Cream Beignets 54
97. Southern Bacon Glazed Green Beans 55
98. Southern Shrimp And Grits 55
99. Southern Style Banana Pudding With Meringue 56
100. Southern Style Crab Cakes With Cool Lime Sauce 56
101. Spiked Peach Iced Tea 57

CHAPTER 5: HAWAIIAN RECIPES......... 57

102. 5 Minute Hot Hawaiian Dip............... 57
103. BBQ Hawaiian Naan Pizza 58
104. Blue Hawaiian Recipe 58
105. Canadian Bacon Hawaiian Pizza Recipe ... 59
106. Easy No Bake Hawaiian Marshmallow Pie 59
107. Grilled Hawaiian Quesadillas 60
108. Ham And Cheese Sandwich Strata...... 60
109. Hawaiian BBQ Glazed Pork Chops 61
110. Hawaiian Chicken Recipe 61
111. Hawaiian Cilantro Lime Chicken Kabobs 62
112. Hawaiian Club Dogs......................... 62
113. Hawaiian Coffee For Two 63
114. Hawaiian Cookie Balls 63
115. Hawaiian Cookies 64
116. Hawaiian Flatbread Appetizer........... 64
117. Hawaiian Jalapeño Bacon Pizza 65
118. Hawaiian Pineapple Spread 65
119. Hawaiian Sausage Sliders 65

120. Hawaiian Tamales 66
121. Luau Meatballs 67
122. Luau Sandwich With Hawaiian Bread 67
123. Mini Crab Sandwich Recipe.............. 67
124. Quick Hawaiian Pork "Kabob" Foil Packages 68
125. Weeknight Hawaiian Pizza 68

CHAPTER 6: MEDITERRANEAN RECIPES 69

126. 5 Layer Greek Dip 69
127. Cedar Planked Mediterranean Chicken 69
128. Cheese Topped Grilled Tomatoes 70
129. Creamy Mediterranean Dip 70
130. Feta Cheese Mediterranean Salad 71
131. Grilled Chicken Pitas 71
132. Mediterranean Bean Salad Recipe..... 72
133. Mediterranean Chicken.................... 72
134. Mediterranean Chicken Recipe 72
135. Mediterranean Chicken And Mushroom Skillet 73
136. Mediterranean Chicken And Sausage Recipe 73
137. Mediterranean Couscous Salad 74
138. Mediterranean Halibut With Mushroom Rice Pilaf... 74
139. Mediterranean Marinated Vegetable Salad 75
140. Mediterranean Mozza Chicken 75
141. Mediterranean Pork Medallions 76
142. Mediterranean Quinoa Salad Recipe .. 76
143. Mediterranean Salmon For Two 77
144. Mediterranean Herbed Scallops Recipe 77
145. Mixed Greens With Mediterranean Vinaigrette.. 78
146. Olive & Cheese Appetizers............... 78
147. Shrimp Kabobs With Olive And Tomato Relish... 79
148. Simple 'Stuffed Artichoke' Appetizer......79
149. Spicy Feta Dip With Roasted Red Peppers 80
150. Zesty Feta And Vegetable Rotini Salad 80

INDEX 81
CONCLUSION 84

Chapter 1: Asian Recipes

***

1. Asian Chicken, Vegetable And Almond Stir Fry

Serving: 0 | Prep: 20mins | Cook: |Ready in: 20mins

Ingredients

- 1/4 cup KRAFT Asian Toasted Sesame Dressing
- 1 Tbsp. lite soy sauce
- 1 Tbsp. honey
- 2 tsp. oil
- 1 lb. boneless skinless chicken breasts, cut into bite-size pieces
- 4-1/2 tsp. minced fresh ginger
- 1 each red and yellow pepper, cut into 1-inch pieces
- 2 cloves garlic, minced
- 2 cups fresh bean sprouts
- 4 green onions, cut into 1-1/2-inch lengths
- 1/4 cup PLANTERS Sliced Almonds

Direction

- Mix first 3 ingredients until blended.
- Heat oil in wok or large nonstick skillet on medium-high heat. Add chicken, ginger and peppers; cook 5 to 6 min. or until chicken is done, stirring frequently and adding garlic for the last minute.
- Add dressing mixture; cook and stir 30 sec. Stir in bean sprouts and onions; top with nuts.

Nutrition Information

- Calories: 290
- Saturated Fat: 2 g
- Sodium: 380 mg
- Total Fat: 12 g
- Fiber: 3 g
- Sugar: 0 g
- Cholesterol: 65 mg
- Total Carbohydrate: 0 g
- Protein: 29 g

2. Asian Pork & Vegetable Stir Fry For Two

Serving: 0 | Prep: 25mins | Cook: |Ready in: 25mins

Ingredients

- 2 oz. thin multi-grain spaghetti, uncooked
- 1/4 cup KRAFT Lite Asian Toasted Sesame Dressing
- 1-1/2 tsp. creamy peanut butter
- 1-1/2 tsp. lite soy sauce
- 1 cup fresh sugar snap peas
- 1/2 large red pepper, cut into thin strips, then halved crosswise
- 1/2 lb. pork tenderloin, cut into thin strips
- 2 Tbsp. chopped fresh cilantro
- 2 Tbsp. PLANTERS Unsalted COCKTAIL Peanuts, chopped

Direction

- Cook spaghetti as directed on package, omitting salt.
- Meanwhile, gradually whisk dressing into peanut butter in small bowl. Stir in soy sauce; set aside. Stir-fry vegetables in medium nonstick skillet on medium-high heat 3 min. Add meat; stir-fry 3 to 4 min. or until done. Add dressing mixture; stir-fry 2 min. or until slightly thickened.
- Drain spaghetti; place on platter. Top with meat mixture, cilantro and nuts.

Nutrition Information

- Calories: 390
- Protein: 32 g
- Cholesterol: 60 mg
- Total Fat: 13 g
- Sugar: 0 g
- Saturated Fat: 2.5 g
- Fiber: 7 g
- Sodium: 490 mg
- Total Carbohydrate: 0 g

3. Asparagus Beef Ramen Bowl

Serving: 4 | Prep: 25mins | Cook: | Ready in: 25mins

Ingredients

- 1/4 lb. thin whole wheat spaghetti, uncooked
- 1/2 lb. fresh asparagus spears, cut diagonally into 1-inch lengths
- 1/2 red pepper, cut into thin strips
- 1 carrot, sliced
- 1 lb. boneless beef sirloin steak, cut into thin strips
- 2 cloves garlic, minced
- 1/4 cup KRAFT Asian Toasted Sesame Dressing, divided
- 2 Tbsp. HEINZ Ketchup Blended with Sriracha Flavor
- 1 Tbsp. lite soy sauce

Direction

- Cook spaghetti in large saucepan as directed on package, omitting salt and adding vegetables to the boiling water for the last 2 min.
- Meanwhile, heat large heavy nonstick skillet on medium-high heat. Add half the meat; cook 2 to 3 min. or until evenly browned, stirring occasionally. Remove from skillet. Repeat with remaining meat. Return all meat to skillet. Stir in garlic and 2 Tbsp. dressing; cook 2 min. or until slightly thickened, stirring frequently.
- Drain spaghetti mixture. Mix ketchup, soy sauce and remaining dressing until blended. Add to meat mixture in skillet along with the spaghetti mixture; cook 2 to 3 min. or until heated through, stirring frequently.

Nutrition Information

- Calories: 390
- Sodium: 310 mg
- Protein: 30 g
- Fiber: 5 g
- Saturated Fat: 6 g
- Cholesterol: 80 mg
- Sugar: 6 g
- Total Fat: 17 g
- Total Carbohydrate: 31 g

4. Better Than Takeout Moo Shu Pork

Serving: 4 | Prep: 25mins | Cook: 30mins | Ready in: 55mins

Ingredients

- 1 lb. pork tenderloin
- 1/2 cup LEA & PERRINS Marinade Asian Style BBQ
- 3 green onions
- 1 Tbsp. oil
- 3 cups coleslaw blend (cabbage slaw mix)
- 6 oz. cremini mushrooms, sliced
- 8 flour tortillas (6 inch)

Direction

- Cut meat into 1/2-inch-thick slices, then cut each slice into thin strips. Place in shallow dish. Add marinade; stir to evenly coat meat with marinade. Refrigerate 30 min. to marinate.
- Slice onions, keeping white and green pieces separated. Heat oil in large skillet on medium-

high heat. Add meat; cook and stir 5 min. Add coleslaw blend, mushrooms and white onion pieces; cook 5 min. or until meat is done and coleslaw blend is wilted, stirring frequently. Meanwhile, warm tortillas as directed on package.
- Spoon meat mixture onto tortillas; top with green onion pieces.

Nutrition Information

- Calories: 590
- Cholesterol: 60 mg
- Sugar: 17 g
- Fiber: 10 g
- Saturated Fat: 6 g
- Protein: 33 g
- Total Fat: 19 g
- Total Carbohydrate: 69 g
- Sodium: 1470 mg

5. Bibimbap (Korean Mixed Rice)

Serving: 0 | Prep: 15mins | Cook: 16mins | Ready in: 31mins

Ingredients

- 8 slices OSCAR MAYER Bacon
- 1/2 cup KRAFT Asian Toasted Sesame Dressing, divided
- 2 tsp. oil
- 4 eggs
- 3 cups hot cooked jasmine rice
- 1 cup shredded carrots
- 1 cup thin English cucumber slices, cut in half
- 1/2 cup chopped kimchi
- 2 green onions, sliced

Direction

- Heat oven to 400°F.
- Place bacon in single layer on foil-covered rimmed baking sheet. Remove 4 tsp. dressing; brush evenly onto bacon slices. Bake 14 to 16 min. or until crisp. Drain on paper towel-covered plate.
- Meanwhile, heat oil in large nonstick skillet on medium-high heat. Slip cracked eggs, one at a time, into skillet; cover. Cook on medium-low heat 2 to 4 min. or until whites are set and yolks are cooked to desired doneness. Remove from heat.
- Combine rice with 1/4 cup of the remaining dressing; spoon into 4 serving bowls. Cut each slice of bacon into 4 pieces; place in mound over rice mixture. Add mounds of carrots, cucumbers, kimchi, eggs and onions. Drizzle with remaining dressing.

Nutrition Information

- Calories: 420
- Total Carbohydrate: 41 g
- Sugar: 8 g
- Cholesterol: 205 mg
- Sodium: 840 mg
- Fiber: 2 g
- Protein: 17 g
- Total Fat: 21 g
- Saturated Fat: 5 g

6. Easy Chicken Skewers With Peanut Sauce

Serving: 0 | Prep: 10mins | Cook: 18mins | Ready in: 28mins

Ingredients

- 1/4 cup KRAFT Classic CATALINA Dressing
- 3 Tbsp. creamy peanut butter
- 1 Tbsp. soy sauce
- 1 lb. boneless skinless chicken breasts, cut lengthwise into strips
- 2 Tbsp. PLANTERS Dry Roasted Peanuts, chopped
- 1 green onion, chopped

Direction

- Mix first 3 ingredients in large bowl until well blended. Add chicken; toss to coat. Refrigerate 10 min.
- Heat broiler. Remove chicken from marinade; discard marinade. Thread chicken onto 8 skewers. Place on rack of broiler pan.
- Broil, 6 inches from heat, 4 min. on each side or until chicken is done. Top with nuts and onions.

Nutrition Information

- Calories: 260
- Cholesterol: 65 mg
- Protein: 28 g
- Sodium: 530 mg
- Saturated Fat: 2.5 g
- Total Carbohydrate: 0 g
- Fiber: 1 g
- Sugar: 0 g
- Total Fat: 13 g

7. Easy Chicken Teriyaki Recipe

Serving: 4 | Prep: 10mins | Cook: 25mins | Ready in: 35mins

Ingredients

- 1 Tbsp. oil
- 1 lb. boneless skinless chicken breasts, cut into strips
- 1-1/2 cups water
- 1/3 cup teriyaki sauce
- 1/2 tsp. garlic powder
- 2 cups instant brown rice, uncooked
- 2 cups frozen broccoli florets
- 1/3 cup PLANTERS Salted Peanuts

Direction

- Heat oil in large nonstick skillet on medium-high heat. Add chicken; cook and stir 5 to 7 min. or until done.
- Add next 3 ingredients; stir. Bring to boil.
- Stir in remaining ingredients; cover. Cook on low heat 5 min. Remove from heat. Let stand 5 min. Fluff with fork.

Nutrition Information

- Calories: 420
- Sodium: 1070 mg
- Saturated Fat: 2.5 g
- Fiber: 4 g
- Total Fat: 14 g
- Cholesterol: 65 mg
- Sugar: 0 g
- Total Carbohydrate: 0 g
- Protein: 34 g

8. General Tso Chicken

Serving: 4 | Prep: 30mins | Cook: | Ready in: 30mins

Ingredients

- 2 Tbsp. cornstarch
- 1/4 tsp. ground black pepper
- 1 lb. boneless skinless chicken thighs, cut into bite-size pieces
- 1 cup fat-free reduced-sodium chicken broth
- 2 Tbsp. HEINZ Ketchup Blended with Sriracha Flavor
- 1 Tbsp. brown sugar
- 1 Tbsp. seasoned rice vinegar
- 4 tsp. lite soy sauce
- 2 tsp. LEA & PERRINS Worcestershire Sauce
- 1 tsp. chili-garlic sauce
- 2 Tbsp. KRAFT Asian Toasted Sesame Dressing
- 2 cloves garlic, minced
- 1 Tbsp. dry sherry
- 4 dried Thai red chiles
- 2 Tbsp. minced gingerroot

- 1 tsp. orange zest
- 2 green onions, diagonally sliced
- 1/4 cup chopped PLANTERS COCKTAIL Peanuts, toasted

Direction

- Mix cornstarch and pepper. Coat chicken with cornstarch mixture; set aside. Combine broth, ketchup, sugar, vinegar, soy sauce, Worcestershire sauce and chili-garlic sauce in medium bowl.
- Heat dressing in large skillet on medium-high heat. Add chicken and garlic; cook 3 to 4 min. or until chicken is no longer pink. Add sherry, dried chiles, ginger and zest; cook 1 min.
- Stir in broth mixture; cook 6 to 8 min. or until mixture becomes slightly sticky and thickened and chicken is done, stirring occasionally. Serve topped with onions and nuts.

Nutrition Information

- Calories: 280
- Saturated Fat: 2.5 g
- Cholesterol: 100 mg
- Sugar: 0 g
- Protein: 23 g
- Sodium: 810 mg
- Total Carbohydrate: 0 g
- Fiber: 2 g
- Total Fat: 13 g

9. Grilled Teriyaki Chicken With Ramen Noodles

Serving: 4 | Prep: 30mins | Cook: 1hours | Ready in: 1hours30mins

Ingredients

- 1/2 cup KRAFT Asian Toasted Sesame Dressing
- 1/4 cup lite soy sauce
- 2 Tbsp. brown sugar
- 2 Tbsp. minced gingerroot
- 4 cloves garlic, minced
- 4 small boneless skinless chicken breasts (1 lb.)
- 2 pkg. (3 oz. each) ramen noodle soup mix, any flavor
- 1 pkg. (16 oz.) refrigerated pre-cut mixed stir-fry vegetables (broccoli, carrots, green and red peppers, onions, snow peas)
- 2-1/2 cups fat-free reduced-sodium chicken broth
- 1/4 cup PLANTERS Dry Roasted Peanuts

Direction

- Combine first 5 ingredients. Pour 1/4 cup dressing mixture over chicken in shallow dish; turn to evenly coat both sides of breasts with dressing mixture. Refrigerate 1 hour to marinate. Meanwhile, refrigerate remaining dressing mixture until ready to use.
- Heat grill to medium heat. Insert tip of sharp knife into one short side of each block of Noodles; use to split block horizontally in half to make 2 layers. Discard Seasoning Packets or reserve for another use. Place noodles, in single layer, on center of prepared foil sheet; top with vegetables. Bring up sides of foil sheet, leaving opening at top.
- Combine broth and 1/3 cup of the remaining dressing mixture; pour over vegetables and noodles. Fold foil to make packet.
- Remove chicken from marinade; discard marinade. Grill chicken 8 min. on each side or until done (165°F), turning and brushing occasionally with remaining dressing mixture. Meanwhile, place foil packet on grill grate next to chicken; grill 12 to 14 min. or until vegetables are crisp-tender.
- Remove packet from grill. Cut slits in foil to release steam before carefully opening packet; sprinkle vegetables with nuts. Serve with the chicken.

Nutrition Information

- Calories: 490

- Cholesterol: 60 mg
- Sugar: 18 g
- Fiber: 4 g
- Sodium: 960 mg
- Total Carbohydrate: 64 g
- Total Fat: 14 g
- Protein: 26 g
- Saturated Fat: 2 g

10. Indian Style Sunehari Salmon

Serving: 6 | Prep: 15mins | Cook: 20mins | Ready in: 35mins

Ingredients

- 1 skinless salmon fillet (1-1/2 lb.)
- 1/4 cup BULL'S-EYE Original Barbecue Sauce
- 1 tsp. dried fenugreek leaves
- 1 tsp. each garam masala, ground coriander and ground cumin
- 1/2 tsp. ground red pepper (cayenne)
- 1 Tbsp. zest and 1/4 cup juice from 2 lemons, divided
- 12 RITZ Crackers, finely crushed (about 1/2 cup)

Direction

- Heat oven to 400°F.
- Place fish in shallow parchment-lined pan. Mix barbecue sauce and dry seasonings until blended. Stir in 2 Tbsp. lemon juice; brush over fish.
- Combine cracker crumbs and lemon zest; sprinkle over fish.
- Bake 20 min. or until fish flakes easily with fork. Drizzle with remaining lemon juice.

Nutrition Information

- Calories: 210
- Saturated Fat: 2 g
- Sugar: 0 g

- Cholesterol: 55 mg
- Fiber: 1 g
- Sodium: 380 mg
- Total Carbohydrate: 0 g
- Protein: 22 g
- Total Fat: 9 g

11. Japanese Cucumber Salad

Serving: 0 | Prep: 15mins | Cook: | Ready in: 15mins

Ingredients

- 6 baby English cucumbers, cut into 1/4-inch-thick slices
- 1/2 cup slivered red onions
- 1/2 cup shredded carrots
- 1/4 cup KRAFT Asian Toasted Sesame Dressing
- 2 Tbsp. unseasoned rice vinegar
- 1 Tbsp. fresh lime juice
- 1/4 cup PLANTERS Dry Roasted Peanuts, chopped
- 1 Tbsp. sesame seed

Direction

- Combine vegetables in large bowl.
- Whisk dressing, vinegar and lime juice until blended. Add to vegetables; mix lightly.
- Sprinkle with nuts and sesame seed.

Nutrition Information

- Calories: 80
- Total Fat: 4 g
- Sugar: 0 g
- Cholesterol: 0 mg
- Fiber: 2 g
- Total Carbohydrate: 0 g
- Saturated Fat: 0.5 g
- Protein: 3 g
- Sodium: 170 mg

12. Japanese Pancakes

Serving: 0 | Prep: 40mins | Cook: | Ready in: 40mins

Ingredients

- 1-1/2 cups flour
- 3 Tbsp. powdered sugar
- 1 tsp. CALUMET Baking Powder
- 1/2 tsp. salt
- 3 egg whites and 1 egg yolk, divided
- 1-1/4 cups milk
- 1/4 cup butter, melted
- 1/2 cup egg white
- 1 tsp. vanilla
- 1/4 tsp. cream of tartar
- 1/4 cup BAKER'S Semi-Sweet Chocolate Chips
- 1/4 cup whipping cream

Direction

- Combine flour, sugar, baking powder and salt in large bowl; set aside. Whisk egg yolk, milk, butter and vanilla in medium bowl until blended. Add to flour mixture; stir just until blended. (Some lumps may remain.)
- Beat egg whites and cream of tartar in small bowl with mixer on high speed 2 to 3 min. or until stiff peaks form. Fold into pancake batter just until blended. (See tip.)
- Spray insides of 4 (3-inch diameter and 2-1/2-inch-deep) ring molds with cooking spray. Heat large nonstick skillet on medium-low heat; spray with additional cooking spray. Place ring molds in prepared skillet; ladle 1/2 cup batter into each mold. Cover with lid. Cook 5 to 7 min. or until bubbles form on tops of pancakes and batter rises to tops of molds.
- Slide spatula under each filled ring mold, then grasp side of mold with tongs and quickly flip pancake and mold over; cover. Cook 3 to 5 min. or until bottoms of pancakes are golden brown. Transfer pancakes to serving plate; carefully remove molds. Cover pancakes to keep warm. Repeat with remaining batter to make 4 additional pancakes.
- Microwave chocolate chips and cream in microwaveable bowl on HIGH 1 min.; stir until chocolate is completely melted. Serve spooned over the pancakes.

Nutrition Information

- Calories: 240
- Fiber: 1 g
- Total Carbohydrate: 25 g
- Protein: 6 g
- Total Fat: 12 g
- Cholesterol: 50 mg
- Sodium: 290 mg
- Saturated Fat: 7 g
- Sugar: 9 g

13. Matcha Shortbread Cookies

Serving: 0 | Prep: 15mins | Cook: 47mins | Ready in: 1hours2mins

Ingredients

- 3/4 cup flour
- 2 Tbsp. cornstarch
- 1 tsp. green tea powder
- 1/2 cup butter, softened
- 4 oz. (1/2 of 8-oz. pkg.) PHILADELPHIA Cream Cheese, softened
- 1/2 cup powdered sugar
- 1/2 tsp. vanilla
- 2 oz. BAKER'S Semi-Sweet Chocolate, finely chopped

Direction

- Combine flour, cornstarch and tea powder. Beat butter, cream cheese and sugar in large bowl with mixer until blended. Add vanilla; mix well. Gradually add flour mixture, mixing well after each addition. Stir in chocolate.

- Refrigerate 30 min.
- Heat oven to 325°F. Roll dough into 24 (1-inch) balls; place, 2 inches apart, on 2 baking sheets. Flatten to 1/4-inch thickness.
- Bake 10 to 12 min. or until bottoms of cookies are golden brown. Cool on baking sheets 1 min. Remove to wire racks; cool completely.

Nutrition Information

- Calories: 180
- Fiber: less than 1 g
- Cholesterol: 30 mg
- Sugar: 0 g
- Total Fat: 12 g
- Sodium: 85 mg
- Total Carbohydrate: 0 g
- Saturated Fat: 8 g
- Protein: 2 g

14. Matcha Truffles

Serving: 0 | Prep: 20mins | Cook: 1hours10mins | Ready in: 1hours30mins

Ingredients

- 1 pkg. (8 oz.) PHILADELPHIA Cream Cheese, softened
- 2 Tbsp. butter, softened
- 1/2 cup graham cracker crumbs
- 1/4 cup powdered sugar
- 2-1/4 tsp. green tea powder, divided
- 2 pkg. (4 oz. each) BAKER'S White Chocolate, broken into small pieces

Direction

- Beat cream cheese and butter in large bowl with mixer until creamy. Add graham crumbs, sugar and 2 tsp. tea powder; mix well.
- Scoop cream cheese mixture into 28 (1-inch) balls, using about 1 Tbsp. cream cheese mixture for each ball. Place on waxed paper-covered baking sheet. Freeze 10 min.
- Melt chocolate as directed on package. Dip cream cheese balls, 1 at a time, into melted chocolate, turning until evenly coated with chocolate. Return to baking sheet; sprinkle with remaining tea powder.
- Refrigerate 1 hour or until firm.

Nutrition Information

- Calories: 170
- Total Carbohydrate: 14 g
- Protein: 2 g
- Fiber: 0 g
- Total Fat: 12 g
- Saturated Fat: 7 g
- Sodium: 105 mg
- Cholesterol: 30 mg
- Sugar: 12 g

15. Omurice (Japanese Stir Fried Rice With Eggs)

Serving: 0 | Prep: 30mins | Cook: | Ready in: 30mins

Ingredients

- 8 slices OSCAR MAYER Bacon, cut into 1/2-inch-thick slices
- 1/2 cup each chopped green peppers and onions
- 3 cups cooked medium-grain white rice, cooled
- 1 tsp. lite soy sauce
- 6 Tbsp. HEINZ Tomato Ketchup, divided
- 1 tsp. oil
- 6 eggs, beaten

Direction

- Cook and stir bacon and vegetables in large nonstick skillet on medium-high heat 5 min. or until vegetables are crisp-tender.

- Add rice; stir. Cook 3 min., stirring frequently. Add soy sauce and 1/4 cup (4 Tbsp.) ketchup; cook and stir 1 min. Spoon onto serving plate; spread into oval-shaped mound on plate.
- Wash and dry skillet. Heat oil in skillet on medium heat. Add eggs; cook 15 sec., stirring constantly. Tilt skillet to evenly spread eggs onto bottom of skillet. Cook, without stirring, 3 min. or just until eggs are softly set.
- Slip eggs from skillet over rice. Serve topped with remaining ketchup.

Nutrition Information

- Calories: 300
- Sugar: 0 g
- Sodium: 480 mg
- Saturated Fat: 3.5 g
- Protein: 13 g
- Total Carbohydrate: 0 g
- Fiber: 0.7168 g
- Total Fat: 11 g
- Cholesterol: 200 mg

16. Simple Thai Peanut Pork

Serving: 4 | Prep: 15mins | Cook: | Ready in: 15mins

Ingredients

- 4 bone-in pork chops (1-1/2 lb.), 1/2 inch thick
- 1 pkg. (16 oz.) frozen Asian-style stir-fry vegetables
- 1/3 cup A.1. Supreme Garlic Steak Sauce
- 3 Tbsp. creamy peanut butter

Direction

- Heat large nonstick skillet on medium-high heat. Add chops; cook 4 min.
- Turn chops. Add vegetables; cover. Cook 4 to 5 min. or until chops are done (145ºF).
- Transfer chops to plate; cover to keep warm. Add steak sauce and peanut butter to vegetables in skillet; cook and stir 1 to 2 min. or until vegetable mixture is heated through and vegetables are evenly coated with sauce. Spoon over chops.

Nutrition Information

- Calories: 300
- Total Fat: 12 g
- Fiber: 3 g
- Protein: 28 g
- Total Carbohydrate: 0 g
- Cholesterol: 60 mg
- Saturated Fat: 3.5 g
- Sugar: 0 g
- Sodium: 480 mg

17. Sizzling Vegetable Salad

Serving: 8 | Prep: 30mins | Cook: 30mins | Ready in: 1hours

Ingredients

- Glazed Walnuts
- 6 Tbsp. sugar
- 2 Tbsp. water
- 1 Tbsp. brown sugar
- 1 Tbsp. lite soy sauce
- 2 tsp. LEA & PERRINS Worcestershire Sauce
- 1/2 tsp. vanilla
- 1/8 tsp. garlic powder
- 1 dash Chinese five-spice powder
- 1 cup PLANTERS Walnut Halves, toasted
- Grilled Marinated Vegetables
- 4 baby bok choy (1/2 lb.), halved
- 1/2 lb. fresh asparagus spears
- 2 portobello mushrooms, stems and gills removed, cut into 1/2-inch-thick slices
- 1 red pepper, cut into 8 pieces
- 2 baby eggplants (1/2 lb.), cut into 1/2-inch-thick slices
- 1/4 cup canola oil
- 2 Tbsp. HEINZ Balsamic Vinegar

- Dressing
- 3 Tbsp. rice wine vinegar
- 3 Tbsp. lite soy sauce
- 4-1/2 tsp. LEA & PERRINS Worcestershire Sauce
- 2 tsp. chopped fresh cilantro
- 1 small clove garlic
- 2/3 cup canola oil
- 8 cups tightly packed torn mixed salad greens

Direction

- Glazed Walnuts
- Bring all ingredients except nuts to boil in medium saucepan; simmer on medium-low heat 5 to 8 min. or until thickened to syrup-like consistency. Add nuts; stir until evenly coated with syrup. Spread onto rimmed baking sheet sprayed with cooking spray. Cool completely.
- Grilled Marinated Vegetables
- Heat greased grill to medium heat. Combine vegetables in large bowl. Whisk oil and vinegar until blended. Drizzle over vegetables; mix lightly. Grill 6 to 8 min. on each side or until vegetables are crisp-tender. Transfer to large nonstick skillet.
- Dressing
- Blend all ingredients except oil and salad greens in blender until smooth. With blender running, gradually add oil through feed tube at top of blender, continuing to blend until dressing is thickened.
- Assembly
- Add Dressing to Grilled Marinated Vegetables in skillet; cook on medium heat 2 to 3 min. or until heated through, stirring frequently. Cover large platter with salad greens; top with vegetables. Drizzle with any dressing remaining in skillet. Top with Glazed Walnuts.

Nutrition Information

- Calories: 410
- Fiber: 4 g
- Sugar: 15 g
- Protein: 5 g

- Total Fat: 35 g
- Total Carbohydrate: 21 g
- Cholesterol: 5 mg
- Sodium: 360 mg
- Saturated Fat: 3 g

18. Spicy Chicken Yaki Soba Noodle Salad

Serving: 4 | Prep: 20mins | Cook: | Ready in: 20mins

Ingredients

- 1/2 cup KRAFT Asian Toasted Sesame Dressing
- 1 tsp. Sriracha sauce (hot chili sauce)
- 8 oz. soba noodles, uncooked
- 4 small boneless skinless chicken breasts (1 lb.)
- 2 cups shredded napa cabbage
- 1 red pepper, cut into thin strips
- 1 cup shredded carrots
- 1/4 cup PLANTERS Sliced Almonds

Direction

- Heat grill to medium heat.
- Mix dressing and Sriracha sauce until blended. Reserve 2 Tbsp. dressing mixture for brushing onto the chicken. Cook noodles as directed on package.
- Meanwhile, grill chicken 6 to 8 min. on each side or until done (165°F), brushing with reserved dressing mixture for the last 2 min.
- Drain noodles. Rinse with cold water; drain well. Slice chicken.
- Place noodles on 4 plates; top with vegetables, chicken, nuts and remaining dressing mixture.

Nutrition Information

- Calories: 460
- Protein: 34 g
- Sugar: 0 g
- Cholesterol: 65 mg

- Total Carbohydrate: 0 g
- Fiber: 3 g
- Sodium: 880 mg
- Total Fat: 12 g
- Saturated Fat: 2 g

19. Teriyaki Pork Ramen Stir Fry

Serving: 4 | Prep: 30mins | Cook: 30mins | Ready in: 1hours

Ingredients

- 6 Tbsp. LEA & PERRINS Marinade Teriyaki, divided
- 1 lb. boneless pork loin chops, cut into thin strips
- 2 tsp. flour
- 1/4 cup plus 2 Tbsp. water, divided
- 2 pkg. (3 oz. each) ramen noodles, any flavor
- 3 Tbsp. KRAFT Olive Oil Vinaigrettes - Roasted Red Pepper, divided
- 1 pkg. (12 oz.) refrigerated pre-cut mixed stir-fry vegetables (broccoli, carrots, snow peas)

Direction

- Add 3 Tbsp. marinade to meat in shallow dish; stir to evenly coat meat with marinade. Refrigerate 30 min. to marinate. Mix remaining marinade with flour and 1/4 cup water until blended; reserve for later use.
- Break apart Noodles. Add to saucepan of boiling water; stir. Cook 3 min.; drain. Discard Seasoning Packets.
- Heat 2 Tbsp. vinaigrette in large nonstick skillet on medium-high heat. Add vegetables; stir-fry 4 min. Stir in remaining water; bring to boil. Cover; simmer on medium-low heat 2 to 3 min. or until vegetables are crisp-tender. Spoon into bowl; set aside.
- Drain meat; discard marinade. Heat remaining vinaigrette in skillet on medium-high heat. Add meat; stir-fry 3 min. Return vegetables to skillet along with the noodles and reserved marinade mixture; stir-fry 2 to 3 min. or until heated through.

Nutrition Information

- Calories: 430
- Total Fat: 13 g
- Cholesterol: 65 mg
- Saturated Fat: 5 g
- Sugar: 2 g
- Protein: 33 g
- Sodium: 620 mg
- Fiber: 3 g
- Total Carbohydrate: 43 g

20. Teriyaki Steak Skewers

Serving: 0 | Prep: 20mins | Cook: 1hours6mins | Ready in: 1hours26mins

Ingredients

- 1/2 cup A.1. Original Sauce
- 2 Tbsp. soy sauce
- 2 Tbsp. packed brown sugar
- 2 cloves garlic, minced
- 1 tsp. ground ginger
- 1 boneless beef sirloin steak (1 lb.), cut into thin strips
- 2 red peppers, cut into bite-size pieces
- 2 cups fresh pineapple chunks

Direction

- Mix first 5 ingredients. Place meat in glass bowl. Add 1/4 cup steak sauce mixture; stir to evenly coat meat. Refrigerate 1 hour to marinate, stirring occasionally. Refrigerate remaining steak sauce mixture.
- Heat grill to medium-high heat. Drain meat; discard marinade. Alternately thread meat, pineapple and peppers on 8 skewers.

- Grill 4 to 6 min. or until meat is done, turning and brushing occasionally with remaining steak sauce mixture.

Nutrition Information

- Calories: 340
- Fiber: 3 g
- Sugar: 25 g
- Saturated Fat: 4.5 g
- Cholesterol: 70 mg
- Protein: 23 g
- Total Fat: 12 g
- Sodium: 1080 mg
- Total Carbohydrate: 33 g

21. Teriyaki Glazed Water Chestnuts With Bacon

Serving: 6 | Prep: 10mins | Cook: 12mins | Ready in: 22mins

Ingredients

- 1 pkg. (2.52 oz.) OSCAR MAYER Fully Cooked Bacon
- 12 whole water chestnuts
- 12 green pepper strips
- 2 Tbsp. teriyaki baste & glaze sauce

Direction

- Heat oven to 350°F.
- Wrap bacon around water chestnuts and peppers; secure with wooden toothpicks.
- Place in shallow baking dish; brush with glaze.
- Bake 10 to 12 min. or until heated through. Discard toothpicks before serving.

Nutrition Information

- Calories: 60
- Total Carbohydrate: 6 g
- Fiber: 1 g
- Sugar: 2 g
- Sodium: 240 mg
- Total Fat: 3 g
- Saturated Fat: 1 g
- Protein: 3 g
- Cholesterol: 5 mg

22. Thai Chicken With Sugar Snap Peas

Serving: 4 | Prep: 25mins | Cook: 1hours15mins | Ready in: 1hours40mins

Ingredients

- 3/4 cup KRAFT Zesty Italian Dressing, divided
- 1 lb. boneless skinless chicken breasts, cut into thin strips
- 2 Tbsp. crunchy peanut butter
- 2 Tbsp. honey
- 2 Tbsp. lite soy sauce
- 1/2 tsp. crushed red pepper
- 1/2 lb. thin spaghetti, cooked
- 1 pkg. (8 oz.) fresh sugar snap peas, rinsed

Direction

- Pour 1/4 cup dressing over chicken in medium bowl; mix lightly. Refrigerate 1 hour to marinate.
- Meanwhile, whisk remaining dressing with peanut butter, honey, soy sauce and crushed pepper until blended. Reserve for later use.
- Cook spaghetti as directed on package, omitting salt. While spaghetti is cooking, remove chicken from marinade; discard marinade. Cook and stir chicken in large nonstick skillet on medium heat 5 min. or until chicken is no longer pink. Add peas; cook and stir 3 min. or until chicken is done. Remove skillet from heat.
- Drain spaghetti. Add to chicken mixture along with the reserved dressing mixture; mix lightly.

Nutrition Information

- Calories: 510
- Protein: 29 g
- Sugar: 0 g
- Fiber: 5 g
- Total Carbohydrate: 0 g
- Total Fat: 14 g
- Cholesterol: 55 mg
- Saturated Fat: 2 g
- Sodium: 650 mg

23. Thai Coffee

Serving: 0 | Prep: 5mins | Cook: | Ready in: 5mins

Ingredients

- 1/2 cup ground MAXWELL HOUSE Coffee
- 1/2 cup sweetened condensed milk
- 3 cups cold water

Direction

- Place coffee in filter in brew basket of coffee maker. Pour condensed milk into empty pot of coffee maker.
- Prepare coffee with cold water. When brewing is complete, stir until well blended.
- Pour into 4 large cups or mugs to serve.

Nutrition Information

- Calories: 130
- Saturated Fat: 2 g
- Total Fat: 3 g
- Fiber: 0 g
- Sodium: 40 mg
- Total Carbohydrate: 23 g
- Cholesterol: 10 mg
- Sugar: 23 g
- Protein: 3 g

24. Thai Curried Tilapia Skillet

Serving: 4 | Prep: 25mins | Cook: 12mins | Ready in: 37mins

Ingredients

- 1 cup snow peas
- 1 cup matchlike carrot sticks
- 1 red pepper, cut into thin strips
- 1 onion, thinly sliced
- 2 cloves garlic, minced
- 2 tsp. minced gingerroot
- 1/2 cup canned lite coconut milk
- 1/2 cup water
- 1/3 cup PHILADELPHIA 1/3 Less Fat than Cream Cheese
- 1 Tbsp. lite soy sauce
- 1 Tbsp. Thai yellow curry paste
- 4 tilapia fillets (1 lb.)
- 3 cups hot cooked brown basmati rice

Direction

- Cook vegetables, garlic and ginger in large saucepan sprayed with cooking spray on medium-high heat 2 to 3 min. or until vegetables are crisp-tender, stirring frequently.
- Add next 5 ingredients; stir. Bring to boil. Add fish; cover. Simmer on medium-low heat 10 to 12 min. or until fish flakes easily with fork.
- Serve over rice.

Nutrition Information

- Calories: 440
- Sugar: 0 g
- Cholesterol: 105 mg
- Total Fat: 12 g
- Saturated Fat: 7 g
- Sodium: 470 mg
- Protein: 32 g
- Fiber: 4 g
- Total Carbohydrate: 0 g

25. Thai Curry Chicken & Rice

Serving: 4 | Prep: 15mins | Cook: 20mins | Ready in: 35mins

Ingredients

- 1 Tbsp. canola oil
- 2 Tbsp. green curry paste
- 1 lb. boneless skinless chicken breasts, cut into bite-size pieces
- 1 small onion, thinly sliced
- 1 each red and green pepper, cut into thin strips, then cut crosswise in half
- 4 oz. (1/2 of 8-oz. pkg.) PHILADELPHIA Cream Cheese, cubed
- 1/4 cup milk
- 1/8 tsp. white pepper
- 2 cups hot cooked long-grain white rice

Direction

- Heat oil in large nonstick skillet on medium heat. Stir in curry paste until well blended. Add chicken and onions; cook and stir 6 to 8 min. or until chicken is done (165°F). Stir in red and green peppers; cook 4 to 5 min. or until crisp-tender.
- Add cream cheese, milk and white pepper; cook until cream cheese is melted and evenly coats chicken and vegetables, stirring frequently.
- Serve over rice.

Nutrition Information

- Calories: 400
- Saturated Fat: 7 g
- Cholesterol: 100 mg
- Sodium: 560 mg
- Protein: 29 g
- Total Fat: 18 g
- Total Carbohydrate: 0 g
- Fiber: 3 g
- Sugar: 0 g

26. Thai Drunken Noodles

Serving: 0 | Prep: 20mins | Cook: | Ready in: 20mins

Ingredients

- 1/2 lb. dry rice noodles, uncooked
- 2 Tbsp. lite soy sauce
- 1 Tbsp. HEINZ Apple Cider Vinegar
- 1-1/2 tsp. brown sugar
- 1 tsp. chili-garlic sauce
- 1/4 cup KRAFT Asian Toasted Sesame Dressing, divided
- 1 small onion, sliced
- 3 cloves garlic, minced
- 2 tomatoes, chopped

Direction

- Cook noodles as directed on package, omitting salt. Meanwhile, mix soy sauce, vinegar, sugar, chili-garlic sauce and 2 Tbsp. dressing until blended.
- Heat remaining dressing in large deep skillet or wok on high heat. Add onions and garlic; cook and stir 2 min. Remove from heat.
- Add tomatoes, noodles and soy sauce mixture; mix lightly.

Nutrition Information

- Calories: 290
- Fiber: 2 g
- Total Fat: 3 g
- Sodium: 360 mg
- Saturated Fat: 0 g
- Cholesterol: 0 mg
- Total Carbohydrate: 0 g
- Protein: 2 g
- Sugar: 0 g

27. Thai Noodle Salad

Serving: 0 | Prep: 15mins | Cook: | Ready in: 15mins

Ingredients

- 1/4 cup crunchy peanut butter
- 1/4 cup MIRACLE WHIP Dressing
- 2 Tbsp. sesame oil
- 2 Tbsp. water
- 2 tsp. lite soy sauce
- 1 clove garlic, minced
- 1/2 tsp. crushed red pepper
- 1/2 lb. rice stick noodles
- 3/4 cup each matchlike-cut carrots, cucumbers and radishes
- 2 Tbsp. chopped fresh cilantro
- 2 Tbsp. chopped PLANTERS Dry Roasted Peanuts

Direction

- Mix first 7 ingredients until blended.
- Cook noodles as directed on package. Drain, then rinse under cold water. Place in large bowl.
- Add peanut sauce and vegetables; mix lightly. Top with cilantro and nuts.

Nutrition Information

- Calories: 440
- Sugar: 6 g
- Protein: 9 g
- Saturated Fat: 3 g
- Total Carbohydrate: 58 g
- Total Fat: 20 g
- Fiber: 5 g
- Sodium: 340 mg
- Cholesterol: 5 mg

28. Thai Peanut Chicken

Serving: 0 | Prep: 15mins | Cook: 16mins | Ready in: 31mins

Ingredients

- 1/4 cup KRAFT Classic CATALINA Dressing, divided
- 1 lb. boneless skinless chicken breasts, cut into strips
- 1-1/2 cups water
- 1 can (14-1/2 oz.) chicken broth
- 2 Tbsp. soy sauce
- 1 Tbsp. creamy peanut butter
- 1/2 lb. thin spaghetti, broken in half, uncooked
- 2 cups broccoli florets
- 2 carrots, thinly sliced

Direction

- Heat 2 Tbsp. dressing in large skillet on medium heat. Add chicken; cook and stir 5 min. or until done.
- Stir in remaining dressing, water, broth, soy sauce and peanut butter. Bring to boil. Add spaghetti. Cover; simmer 5 min.
- Add vegetables; mix lightly. Simmer, covered, 4 to 6 min. or until spaghetti is tender.

Nutrition Information

- Calories: 450
- Cholesterol: 65 mg
- Saturated Fat: 2 g
- Sodium: 1160 mg
- Fiber: 4 g
- Total Fat: 10 g
- Protein: 37 g
- Total Carbohydrate: 0 g
- Sugar: 0 g

29. Thai BBQ Slow Cooker Ribs

Serving: 8 | Prep: 15mins | Cook: 6hours30mins | Ready in: 6hours45mins

Ingredients

- Juice from 1 lime
- 1 Tbsp. brown sugar
- 1/2 tsp. cracked peppercorns
- 1/4 tsp. ground ginger
- 2/3 cup chopped fresh cilantro, divided
- 2 Thai red chiles, divided
- 4 lb. pork baby back ribs, cut into 3-rib sections
- 1/3 cup A.1. Sweet Chili Garlic Sauce
- 1/4 cup KRAFT Original Barbecue Sauce

Direction

- Blend first 4 ingredients, half the cilantro, and 1 red chile in blender until smooth.
- Place ribs in slow cooker. Pour prepared sauce over ribs; cover with lid.
- Cook on LOW 6 to 7 hours (or on HIGH 3 to 4 hours). Remove ribs from slow cooker, discard drippings from slow cooker.
- Return ribs to slow cooker. Mix A.1. and barbecue sauce until blended; brush onto ribs. Cook, covered, on HIGH 30 min.
- Transfer ribs to platter. Cut remaining chile into thin slices; place over ribs. Sprinkle with remaining cilantro.

Nutrition Information

- Calories: 340
- Total Fat: 23 g
- Cholesterol: 90 mg
- Total Carbohydrate: 8 g
- Saturated Fat: 8 g
- Sodium: 380 mg
- Protein: 25 g
- Sugar: 7 g
- Fiber: 0 g

Chapter 2: Chinese Recipes

***

30. Asian Beef Ribs

Serving: 8 | Prep: 20mins | Cook: | Ready in: 20mins

Ingredients

- 1 Tbsp. oil
- 2 tsp. Chinese five-spice powder
- 1 tsp. garlic powder
- 2 lb. boneless beef short ribs
- 1/2 cup A.1. Sweet Chili Garlic Sauce

Direction

- Heat grill to medium-high heat.
- Mix first 3 ingredients until blended. Add to ribs in large bowl; toss to evenly coat.
- Grill 10 to 12 min. or until ribs are done (145°F), turning occasionally and brushing with A.1. for the last few minutes.
- Remove ribs from grill. Let stand 3 min. before serving.

Nutrition Information

- Calories: 250
- Sugar: 5 g
- Cholesterol: 65 mg
- Protein: 21 g
- Fiber: 1 g
- Sodium: 340 mg
- Total Carbohydrate: 7 g
- Saturated Fat: 6 g
- Total Fat: 14 g

31. Asian Meatballs With Lo Mein Noodles

Serving: 0 | Prep: 45mins | Cook: | Ready in: 45mins

Ingredients

- 2 Tbsp. cornstarch
- 1 can (14-1/2 oz.) fat-free reduced-sodium beef broth
- 1/4 cup KRAFT Asian Toasted Sesame Dressing, divided
- 2 Tbsp. soy sauce
- 2 tsp. Chinese five-spice powder, divided
- 1/4 tsp. crushed red pepper
- 1 lb. lean ground beef
- 1/4 cup panko bread crumbs
- 2 pkg. (8 oz. each) wide lo mein noodles
- 1 Tbsp. oil
- 2 carrots, thinly sliced (about 1 cup)
- 1 cup halved snow peas
- 4 green onions, chopped

Direction

- Mix cornstarch and broth until blended. Add 2 Tbsp. dressing, soy sauce, 1 tsp. five-spice powder and crushed pepper; mix well.
- Combine meat, bread crumbs and remaining dressing and five-spice powder; shape into 1-inch balls.
- Cook noodles as directed on package, omitting salt. Meanwhile, heat oil in large skillet on medium-high heat. Add meatballs; cook 10 min. or until evenly browned, stirring occasionally. Remove meatballs from skillet. Add carrots to skillet; cook and stir 4 min. Stir in snow peas and onions; cook and stir 1 min.
- Return meatballs to skillet. Stir in broth mixture. Bring to boil; simmer on medium heat 4 min. or until meatballs are done (160°F) and sauce is slightly thickened, stirring occasionally.
- Drain noodles. Add to ingredients in skillet; stir.

Nutrition Information

- Calories: 340
- Total Fat: 9 g
- Protein: 16 g
- Saturated Fat: 2 g
- Total Carbohydrate: 0 g
- Cholesterol: 30 mg
- Sodium: 620 mg
- Fiber: 2 g
- Sugar: 0 g

32. Asian Peanut Noodles With Beef For Two

Serving: 2 | Prep: 30mins | Cook: | Ready in: 30mins

Ingredients

- 1/4 lb. spaghetti, uncooked, broken in half
- 1-1/2 cups sugar snap peas, trimmed
- 1/2 cup red pepper strips
- 1/4 cup KRAFT Lite CATALINA Dressing
- 1/2 lb. well-trimmed boneless beef sirloin steak, cut into thin strips
- 1 Tbsp. creamy peanut butter
- 1 Tbsp. lite soy sauce
- 2 green onions, sliced
- 1/4 cup chopped PLANTERS Dry Roasted Peanuts

Direction

- Cook spaghetti in large saucepan as directed on package, omitting salt and adding snap peas and pepper strips to the boiling water for the last 2 min.
- Meanwhile, heat dressing in large skillet on medium-high heat. Add meat; stir-fry 3 min. or until meat is barely pink in center. Add peanut butter and soy sauce; stir-fry 1 min. or until sauce is thickened and meat is done.
- Drain spaghetti mixture. Add to meat mixture; mix lightly. Stir in onions; sprinkle with nuts.

Nutrition Information

- Calories: 710
- Sugar: 18 g
- Fiber: 8 g
- Total Carbohydrate: 75 g
- Protein: 43 g
- Cholesterol: 80 mg
- Sodium: 860 mg
- Total Fat: 28 g
- Saturated Fat: 7 g

33. Baked Shrimp Rangoon Appetizers

Serving: 0 | Prep: 20mins | Cook: 20mins | Ready in: 40mins

Ingredients

- 1 green onion, thinly sliced, divided
- 4 oz. (1/2 of 8-oz. pkg.) PHILADELPHIA Cream Cheese, softened
- 1 can (4 oz.) baby shrimp, rinsed
- 2 Tbsp. finely chopped red peppers
- 1/4 cup MIRACLE WHIP Dressing
- 1/2 tsp. hot pepper sauce
- 24 wonton wrappers

Direction

- Heat oven to 350°F.
- Reserve 1 Tbsp. onions. Combine remaining onions with next 5 ingredients.
- Place 1 wonton wrapper in each of 24 mini muffin pan cups sprayed with cooking spray, extending edges of wrapper over rim of cup. Fill with shrimp mixture.
- Bake 18 to 20 min. or until edges of wrappers are golden brown and filling is heated through. Top with reserved onions.

Nutrition Information

- Calories: 100
- Saturated Fat: 2 g
- Sugar: 1 g
- Protein: 4 g
- Sodium: 200 mg
- Total Carbohydrate: 10 g
- Total Fat: 4.5 g
- Cholesterol: 35 mg
- Fiber: 0 g

34. Bok Choy Stir Fry With Shrimp

Serving: 4 | Prep: 20mins | Cook: | Ready in: 20mins

Ingredients

- 1/4 cup KRAFT Zesty Italian Dressing
- 1 tsp. grated gingerroot
- 2 tsp. sugar
- 1 Tbsp. oil
- 1 red pepper, cut into strips
- 1/2 onion, sliced
- 1/2 lb. baby bok choy, cut into 1-inch pieces (about 2 cups)
- 3/4 lb. uncooked deveined peeled medium shrimp

Direction

- Mix first 3 ingredients until blended.
- Heat oil in large skillet on medium-high heat. Add peppers and onions; stir-fry 2 min. Add bok choy; stir-fry 1 min. Transfer to bowl; cover to keep warm.
- Add 1 Tbsp. of the dressing mixture and shrimp to skillet; stir-fry 2 min. Add vegetables and remaining dressing mixture; stir-fry 1 to 2 min. or until shrimp turn pink and vegetables are heated through.

Nutrition Information

- Calories: 180
- Sugar: 5 g

- Total Carbohydrate: 8 g
- Saturated Fat: 0.5 g
- Cholesterol: 150 mg
- Protein: 20 g
- Total Fat: 7 g
- Sodium: 400 mg
- Fiber: 1 g

35. Chicken Lo Mein

Serving: 0 | Prep: 25mins | Cook: |Ready in: 25mins

Ingredients

- 1/2 lb. spaghetti, uncooked
- 1/4 cup KRAFT Asian Toasted Sesame Dressing
- 1 lb. boneless skinless chicken breasts, cut into thin strips
- 2 cloves garlic, minced
- 1 pkg. (16 oz.) frozen bell pepper and onion strips, thawed, drained
- 1/2 cup fat-free reduced-sodium chicken broth
- 1 Tbsp. creamy peanut butter
- 1/4 cup lite soy sauce
- 2 Tbsp. chopped fresh cilantro
- 2 Tbsp. chopped PLANTERS COCKTAIL Peanuts

Direction

- Cook spaghetti in large saucepan as directed on package, omitting salt.
- Meanwhile, heat dressing in large nonstick skillet on medium-high heat. Add chicken and garlic; stir-fry 5 min. or until chicken is no longer pink. Add vegetables, broth and peanut butter; stir-fry 3 to 4 min. or until chicken is done.
- Drain spaghetti; return to pan. Add chicken mixture and soy sauce; mix lightly.
- Spoon onto platter; top with cilantro and nuts.

Nutrition Information

- Calories: 310
- Sugar: 0 g
- Saturated Fat: 1.5 g
- Fiber: 3 g
- Cholesterol: 40 mg
- Total Carbohydrate: 0 g
- Sodium: 420 mg
- Total Fat: 7 g
- Protein: 19 g

36. Chicken Cabbage Noodle Salad

Serving: 0 | Prep: 15mins | Cook: |Ready in: 15mins

Ingredients

- 1/2 cup KRAFT Balsamic Vinaigrette Dressing
- 2 Tbsp. sugar
- 1 Tbsp. lite soy sauce
- 2 pkg. (3 oz. each) ramen noodle soup mix
- 1 cup hot water
- 4 cups coleslaw blend (cabbage slaw mix)
- 2 cups shredded cooked chicken
- 3/4 cup PLANTERS Dry Roasted Peanuts

Direction

- Mix dressing, sugar and soy sauce until blended. Dissolve 1 Seasoning Packet (from ramen soup package) in hot water. Add to dressing mixture; mix well. Discard remaining seasoning packet or reserve for another use.
- Break Ramen Noodles apart; place in large bowl. Add coleslaw blend, chicken and nuts; mix lightly.
- Add dressing mixture; toss to coat.

Nutrition Information

- Calories: 410
- Saturated Fat: 5 g
- Sugar: 9 g
- Protein: 22 g
- Sodium: 670 mg

- Fiber: 3 g
- Cholesterol: 40 mg
- Total Fat: 23 g
- Total Carbohydrate: 30 g

37. Chinese Orange Chicken Recipe

Serving: 0 | Prep: 15mins | Cook: 14mins | Ready in: 29mins

Ingredients

- 1 large navel orange
- 1/4 cup KRAFT Asian Toasted Sesame Dressing
- 2 Tbsp. lite soy sauce
- 2 Tbsp. sugar
- 1/2 tsp. crushed red pepper
- 1 lb. boneless skinless chicken thighs, cut into bite-size pieces
- 1 Tbsp. minced gingerroot
- 1 clove garlic, minced
- 1 large red pepper, cut into bite-size pieces

Direction

- Grate 1 tsp. zest from orange. Use small sharp knife to cut remaining peel and white pith from orange; cut orange into bite-size pieces. Mix zest, dressing, soy sauce, sugar and crushed pepper.
- Cook chicken in nonstick skillet on high heat 5 to 6 min. or until done, stirring frequently. Add ginger and garlic; cook and stir on medium-high heat 2 min. Add red peppers; cook 2 min. or until crisp-tender, stirring frequently. Transfer to bowl; cover to keep warm.
- Add dressing mixture to skillet; cook and stir 1 to 2 min. or until thickened, stirring constantly. Add chicken mixture; cook and stir 2 min. or until heated through. Stir in oranges; spoon onto platter.

Nutrition Information

- Calories: 170
- Sodium: 370 mg
- Fiber: 2 g
- Total Carbohydrate: 19 g
- Sugar: 15 g
- Saturated Fat: 1 g
- Total Fat: 5 g
- Cholesterol: 45 mg
- Protein: 13 g

38. Chinese Shrimp Recipe

Serving: 0 | Prep: 25mins | Cook: 1hours | Ready in: 1hours25mins

Ingredients

- 1 lb. uncooked deveined peeled medium shrimp
- 1 Tbsp. minced fresh ginger
- 2 cloves garlic, minced
- 1/4 cup reduced-sodium teriyaki sauce
- 1/4 cup fat-free reduced-sodium chicken broth
- 1/4 tsp. crushed red pepper
- 2 tsp. olive oil
- 4 cups small broccoli florets
- 2 carrots, thinly sliced
- 1 cup PLANTERS Cashew Halves with Pieces

Direction

- Toss shrimp with ginger and garlic. Refrigerate 1 hour. Meanwhile, mix teriyaki sauce, broth and crushed pepper until blended.
- Heat oil in large skillet. Add shrimp mixture; cook and stir 3 to 5 min. or until shrimp turn pink. Add teriyaki mixture, broccoli and carrots; stir. Cook until vegetables are crisp-tender, stirring frequently.
- Add nuts; mix lightly.

Nutrition Information

- Calories: 260
- Sugar: 0 g
- Protein: 23 g
- Total Carbohydrate: 0 g
- Fiber: 3 g
- Saturated Fat: 2.5 g
- Total Fat: 14 g
- Sodium: 530 mg
- Cholesterol: 135 mg

39. Chinese Takeout Style Lemon Chicken

Serving: 4 | Prep: 25mins | Cook: | Ready in: 25mins

Ingredients

- 1 pkg. (3 oz.) JELL-O Lemon Flavor Gelatin
- 1 Tbsp. cornstarch
- 1/2 cup fat-free reduced-sodium chicken broth
- 2 Tbsp. KRAFT Zesty Italian Dressing
- 2 cloves garlic, minced
- 1 Tbsp. oil
- 1 lb. boneless skinless chicken breasts, cut into thin strips
- 2 cups snow peas (about 6 oz.), trimmed
- 1 red pepper, cut into thin strips
- 2 cups hot cooked long-grain white rice

Direction

- Combine dry gelatin mix and cornstarch in medium bowl. Add broth, dressing and garlic; stir until gelatin is completely dissolved.
- Heat oil in large skillet on medium heat. Add chicken; cook 4 to 5 min. or until done, stirring occasionally. Add snow peas and peppers; cook and stir 2 min.
- Stir gelatin mixture; add to ingredients in skillet. Cook on medium heat 3 min. or until sauce is thickened, stirring frequently. Serve over rice.

Nutrition Information

- Calories: 400
- Protein: 30 g
- Total Carbohydrate: 0 g
- Total Fat: 8 g
- Fiber: 2 g
- Cholesterol: 65 mg
- Sodium: 310 mg
- Saturated Fat: 1.5 g
- Sugar: 0 g

40. Chinese Style Pork Stir Fry

Serving: 4 | Prep: 20mins | Cook: | Ready in: 20mins

Ingredients

- 1 Tbsp. oil
- 1 lb. boneless pork chops, cut into strips
- 2 cups frozen Asian mixed vegetables (carrots, broccoli florets, red pepper strips, sugarsnap peas)
- 1/4 cup KRAFT Zesty Italian Dressing
- 2 Tbsp. lite soy sauce
- 2 Tbsp. honey
- 1/4 tsp. ground ginger
- 2 cups hot cooked long-grain white rice

Direction

- Heat oil in nonstick wok or large nonstick skillet on medium-high heat. Add meat; stir-fry 5 min. or until done.
- Add all remaining ingredients except rice; stir-fry 5 min. or until heated through.
- Serve over rice.

Nutrition Information

- Calories: 350
- Cholesterol: 55 mg
- Sodium: 490 mg
- Fiber: 1 g

- Protein: 26 g
- Total Fat: 10 g
- Sugar: 0 g
- Saturated Fat: 2 g
- Total Carbohydrate: 0 g

41. Coconut Almond Cookies

Serving: 0 | Prep: 20mins | Cook: 9mins | Ready in: 29mins

Ingredients

- 3 cups flour
- 1 cup BAKER'S ANGEL FLAKE Coconut, toasted
- 1-1/2 tsp. baking soda
- 1/2 cup (1 stick) butter, softened
- 1/2 cup shortening
- 1 cup sugar
- 1 egg
- 2 Tbsp. honey
- 2 tsp. almond extract
- 1/2 cup PLANTERS Sliced Almonds

Direction

- Preheat oven to 375°F. Mix flour, coconut and baking soda; set aside. Beat butter and shortening in large bowl with electric mixer on medium speed until well mixed. Add sugar; beat until light and fluffy. Add egg, honey and almond extract; beat until well blended. Gradually add flour mixture, beating on low speed after each addition until well blended.
- Shape level tablespoonfuls of dough into balls. Place, 2 inches apart, on ungreased baking sheets. Flatten each ball with bottom of drinking glass; press almond slice into center of each cookie.
- Bake 9 minutes or until golden brown. Cool 5 minutes; remove from baking sheets. Cool completely on wire racks. Store in tightly covered container at room temperature.

Nutrition Information

- Calories: 230
- Sugar: 13 g
- Cholesterol: 20 mg
- Total Carbohydrate: 28 g
- Protein: 3 g
- Sodium: 140 mg
- Total Fat: 12 g
- Fiber: 1 g
- Saturated Fat: 7 g

42. Crispy Wontons With Asian Dipping Sauce

Serving: 0 | Prep: 25mins | Cook: 12mins | Ready in: 37mins

Ingredients

- 1 tub (8 oz.) PHILADELPHIA Chive & Onion Cream Cheese Spread
- 1/2 lb. ground pork, cooked, well drained
- 1 tsp. minced fresh ginger
- 1 tsp. sesame oil
- 32 wonton wrappers
- 1/4 cup water, divided
- 2 tsp. sesame seed
- 2 Tbsp. soy sauce
- 1 Tbsp. rice wine

Direction

- Heat oven to 425°F.
- Mix first 4 ingredients until blended.
- Spoon 1 Tbsp. meat mixture onto center of each wonton wrapper. Bring corners together over meat mixture, then twist to enclose filling. Place on rimmed baking sheet sprayed with cooking spray; press gently to flatten bottoms slightly. Brush evenly with 3 Tbsp. water; sprinkle with sesame seed.
- Bake 10 to 12 min. or until golden brown. Remove from pan; drain on paper towels.

- Mix soy sauce, rice wine and remaining water until blended; serve with wontons.

Nutrition Information

- Calories: 120
- Cholesterol: 20 mg
- Total Fat: 6 g
- Fiber: 0 g
- Total Carbohydrate: 0 g
- Protein: 5 g
- Saturated Fat: 3 g
- Sodium: 300 mg
- Sugar: 0 g

43. Crunchy Asian Salad

Serving: 0 | Prep: 15mins | Cook: | Ready in: 15mins

Ingredients

- 1 env. (0.7 oz.) GOOD SEASONS Italian Dressing Mix
- 1/2 cup sugar
- 2 Tbsp. lite soy sauce
- 2 pkg. (3 oz. each) ramen noodle soup mix
- 2 pkg. (16 oz. each) coleslaw blend (cabbage slaw mix)
- 4 green onions, sliced
- 1/2 cup PLANTERS Dry Roasted Sunflower Kernels
- 1/2 cup PLANTERS Sliced Almonds, toasted

Direction

- Prepare dressing mix in small bowl as directed on envelope. Stir in sugar and soy sauce.
- Break Noodles apart; place in large bowl. Discard Seasoning Packets or reserve for another use. Add coleslaw blend, onions, sunflower kernels and nuts to noodles; mix lightly.
- Add dressing; toss to evenly coat noodle mixture.

Nutrition Information

- Calories: 260
- Total Fat: 16 g
- Total Carbohydrate: 0 g
- Protein: 5 g
- Fiber: 3 g
- Cholesterol: 0 mg
- Sugar: 0 g
- Saturated Fat: 2.5 g
- Sodium: 370 mg

44. Easy Chicken Stir Fry

Serving: 0 | Prep: 10mins | Cook: 8mins | Ready in: 18mins

Ingredients

- 3 cups fresh stir-fry vegetables (green peppers, mushrooms, broccoli, carrots)
- 1 Tbsp. oil
- 1 pkg. (6 oz.) OSCAR MAYER CARVING BOARD Flame Grilled Chicken Breast Strips
- 1/4 cup stir-fry sauce
- 1-1/2 cups hot cooked long-grain white rice

Direction

- Cook and stir vegetables in hot oil in medium skillet on medium-high heat 5 min. or until crisp-tender.
- Add chicken and sauce; cover. Cook 2 min. or until heated through, stirring occasionally.
- Serve over rice.

Nutrition Information

- Calories: 260
- Sugar: 0 g
- Protein: 19 g
- Total Carbohydrate: 0 g
- Cholesterol: 40 mg

- Saturated Fat: 1.5 g
- Fiber: 3 g
- Sodium: 910 mg
- Total Fat: 6 g

45. Easy Chinese Stir Fry

Serving: 0 | Prep: 30mins | Cook: | Ready in: 30mins

Ingredients

- 1 tsp. oil
- 1 lb. pork tenderloin, cut into thin strips
- 3 carrots, sliced
- 1/3 cup KRAFT Balsamic Vinaigrette Dressing
- 2 Tbsp. hoisin sauce
- 2 green onions, thinly sliced

Direction

- Heat oil in large skillet on medium-high heat. Add meat and carrots; stir-fry 5 min.
- Stir in dressing and hoisin sauce; stir-fry 7 min. or until meat is done and carrots are crisp-tender.
- Add onions; stir-fry 1 min.

Nutrition Information

- Calories: 210
- Sugar: 0 g
- Cholesterol: 60 mg
- Fiber: 2 g
- Sodium: 410 mg
- Total Carbohydrate: 0 g
- Total Fat: 8 g
- Protein: 22 g
- Saturated Fat: 1.5 g

46. Fresh Pineapple Tapioca

Serving: 0 | Prep: 20mins | Cook: 3hours | Ready in: 3hours20mins

Ingredients

- 2-1/2 cups pineapple-orange-banana juice blend
- 1/4 cup MINUTE Tapioca
- 2 Tbsp. butter
- 4 cups fresh pineapple chunks
- 1 Tbsp. firmly packed light brown sugar
- 1/2 tsp. ground nutmeg
- 1/4 tsp. salt
- 1 tub (8 oz.) COOL WHIP Whipped Topping, thawed
- 1 cup BAKER'S ANGEL FLAKE Coconut, toasted

Direction

- Mix juice and tapioca in medium bowl. Let stand 5 minutes. Meanwhile, melt butter in large saucepan on medium heat. Add pineapple, brown sugar, nutmeg and salt; mix well. Cook 5 minutes, stirring frequently.
- Add tapioca mixture; stir. Bring to a full boil, stirring constantly. Remove from heat. Cool 20 minutes. Transfer to serving bowl. Cover and refrigerate several hours or until chilled.
- Spread whipped topping over pudding just before serving; sprinkle with coconut.

Nutrition Information

- Calories: 200
- Fiber: 1 g
- Sugar: 19 g
- Protein: 1 g
- Cholesterol: 5 mg
- Total Fat: 9 g
- Sodium: 115 mg
- Saturated Fat: 8 g
- Total Carbohydrate: 28 g

47. Orange Ginger Beef Stir Fry

Serving: 0 | Prep: 10mins | Cook: 11mins | Ready in: 21mins

Ingredients

- 1 lb. beef flank steak, cut into strips
- 2 tsp. cornstarch
- 3 Tbsp. orange marmalade
- 3/4 tsp. ground ginger
- 1 Tbsp. canola oil
- 1 pkg. (10 oz.) frozen broccoli florets, thawed
- 1 can (8 oz.) sliced water chestnuts, drained
- 1/4 cup lite soy sauce
- 2 cups hot cooked long-grain brown rice
- 1/4 cup PLANTERS Dry Roasted Peanuts

Direction

- Toss meat with cornstarch in medium bowl. Add marmalade and ginger; stir until well blended.
- Heat oil in large nonstick skillet on medium-high heat. Add meat mixture; stir-fry 4 to 5 min. or until meat is done. Add broccoli, water chestnuts and soy sauce; mix well. Cover; simmer on medium-low heat 5 min. or until thickened, stirring frequently.
- Serve over rice; top with nuts.

Nutrition Information

- Calories: 460
- Sodium: 640 mg
- Saturated Fat: 4 g
- Total Carbohydrate: 0 g
- Protein: 31 g
- Total Fat: 16 g
- Cholesterol: 45 mg
- Fiber: 6 g
- Sugar: 0 g

48. Shrimp Fried Rice Recipe

Serving: 4 | Prep: 20mins | Cook: | Ready in: 20mins

Ingredients

- 2 Tbsp. oil
- 3/4 cup chopped OSCAR MAYER Smoked Ham
- 3/4 cup sliced fresh mushrooms
- 1/2 cup frozen peas
- 2 green onions, sliced
- 1/2 lb. frozen uncooked cleaned medium shrimp, thawed
- 1-1/2 cups chilled cooked long-grain white rice
- 3 Tbsp. lite soy sauce
- 1 egg, beaten

Direction

- Heat oil in large nonstick skillet on medium-high heat. Add ham and vegetables; stir-fry 4 min.
- Add shrimp; stir-fry 4 min. or until shrimp turn pink.
- Add remaining ingredients; stir-fry 2 to 3 min. or until egg is set and ham mixture is heated through.

Nutrition Information

- Calories: 270
- Total Carbohydrate: 0 g
- Sodium: 1160 mg
- Protein: 20 g
- Total Fat: 10 g
- Saturated Fat: 2 g
- Sugar: 0 g
- Fiber: 1 g
- Cholesterol: 155 mg

49. Sizzling Shrimp Stir Fry

Serving: 0 | Prep: 15mins | Cook: 15mins | Ready in: 30mins

Ingredients

- 2 tsp. cornstarch
- 1 Tbsp. lite soy sauce
- 1/2 cup fat-free reduced-sodium chicken broth
- 1/4 cup KRAFT Lite Zesty Italian Dressing, divided
- 1 lb. uncooked large shrimp, peeled, deveined
- 1 Tbsp. grated gingerroot
- 2 cloves garlic, minced
- 2 cups sliced baby bok choy
- 1 cup sugar snap peas
- 4 green onions, diagonally cut into 1/2-inch lengths
- 1/2 cup cherry tomatoes, halved
- 2-2/3 cups hot cooked long-grain brown rice

Direction

- Mix cornstarch and soy sauce until blended. Stir in broth and 2 Tbsp. dressing.
- Heat remaining dressing in large skillet on medium-high heat. Add shrimp, ginger and garlic; stir-fry 3 min. or until shrimp turn pink. Add bok choy; stir-fry 2 min. Add peas and onions; stir-fry 2 to 3 min. or until crisp-tender. Stir in soy sauce mixture; bring to boil, stirring constantly. Simmer on medium heat 1 to 2 min. or until thickened, stirring frequently.
- Add tomatoes; cook and stir 1 min. or until heated through. Serve over rice.

Nutrition Information

- Calories: 310
- Sugar: 3 g
- Total Fat: 3.5 g
- Saturated Fat: 1 g
- Total Carbohydrate: 39 g
- Protein: 28 g
- Sodium: 1360 mg
- Fiber: 4 g
- Cholesterol: 210 mg

50. Speedy Ginger Chicken Soup Bowls

Serving: 4 | Prep: 15mins | Cook: | Ready in: 15mins

Ingredients

- 3/4 cup instant white rice, uncooked
- 4 mL minced fresh ginger
- 1 mL OSCAR MAYER CARVING BOARD Flame Grilled Chicken Breast Strips
- 2 mL cut-up fresh vegetables (thin red pepper strips, sliced carrots and sliced green onions)
- 2 mL fat-free reduced-sodium chicken broth
- 2 cups water

Direction

- Combine 3 Tbsp. rice and 1 tsp. ginger in each of 4 microwaveable soup bowls.
- Top each with 1/4 cup chicken and 1/2 cup vegetables; stir.
- Add 1/2 cup each broth and water to each bowl; cover with waxed paper. Microwave on HIGH 2 min. Let stand 5 min. before serving.

Nutrition Information

- Calories: 130
- Total Carbohydrate: 0 g
- Sugar: 0 g
- Protein: 11 g
- Sodium: 420 mg
- Total Fat: 1 g
- Cholesterol: 25 mg
- Fiber: 2 g
- Saturated Fat: 0 g

51. Szechuan Beef Stir Fry

Serving: 0 | Prep: 25mins | Cook: | Ready in: 25mins

Ingredients

- 1 boneless beef sirloin steak (1 lb.), well trimmed
- 3 cloves garlic, minced
- 1/4 tsp. crushed red pepper
- 1/4 cup KRAFT Lite Asian Toasted Sesame Dressing
- 2 Tbsp. hoisin sauce
- 2 Tbsp. lite soy sauce
- 2 tsp. cornstarch
- 2 tsp. oil
- 1 cup matchlike carrot sticks
- 2 stalks celery, thinly sliced
- 3 large green onions, sliced

Direction

- Cut steak crosswise into thin slices, then cut each slice into thin strips. Place meat in medium bowl. Add garlic and crushed pepper; mix lightly. Combine next 4 ingredients.
- Heat oil in large skillet on medium-high heat. Add meat, in batches; stir-fry 1 to 2 min. or just until meat strips are no longer pink in centers. Transfer to plate; set aside.
- Add carrots and celery to skillet; stir-fry 2 min. Return meat to skillet along with the dressing mixture; stir-fry 1 to 2 min. or until meat is done and sauce is slightly thickened. Stir in onions.

Nutrition Information

- Calories: 230
- Fiber: 2 g
- Total Fat: 9 g
- Sodium: 630 mg
- Cholesterol: 60 mg
- Total Carbohydrate: 0 g
- Protein: 22 g
- Saturated Fat: 2.5 g
- Sugar: 0 g

52. Tofu Stir Fry Recipe

Serving: 4 | Prep: 10mins | Cook: 25mins | Ready in: 35mins

Ingredients

- 1 pkg. (14 oz.) firm tofu, drained, cut into 1/2-inch cubes
- 1/4 cup flour
- 1 Tbsp. oil
- 1/2 cup KRAFT Balsamic Vinaigrette Dressing
- 3 Tbsp. lite soy sauce
- 1-1/2 cups chopped cabbage
- 1 cup fresh green beans, trimmed, cut in half
- 1/2 cup each: sliced onions and carrots
- 2-2/3 cups hot cooked brown rice

Direction

- Toss tofu with flour in small bowl until evenly coated. Heat oil in large skillet on medium-high heat. Add tofu; cook 8 min. or until lightly browned on all sides, stirring occasionally. Remove from skillet; cover to keep warm.
- Mix dressing and soy sauce until well blended. Add 2 Tbsp. of the dressing mixture, vegetables and soy beans to same skillet; cook and stir 10 min. or until vegetables are crisp-tender.
- Add remaining dressing mixture and the tofu to vegetable mixture; mix lightly. Cook 2 min., stirring gently. Serve over the rice.

Nutrition Information

- Calories: 350
- Total Fat: 9 g
- Cholesterol: 0 mg
- Sugar: 0 g
- Saturated Fat: 1.5 g

- Total Carbohydrate: 0 g
- Sodium: 490 mg
- Protein: 17 g
- Fiber: 5 g

53. Wonton Soup

Serving: 0 | Prep: 55mins | Cook: | Ready in: 55mins

Ingredients

- 4 green onions, divided
- 1-1/2 cups sliced shiitake mushrooms, divided
- 1 can (8 oz.) sliced water chestnuts, drained, divided
- 1/2 lb. ground pork
- 2 Tbsp. KRAFT Asian Toasted Sesame Dressing
- 1 egg, separated
- 32 wonton wrappers
- 2 qt. (8 cups) fat-free reduced-sodium chicken broth

Direction

- Chop 2 onions. Finely chop enough mushrooms to measure 1/4 cup and enough water chestnuts to measure 2 Tbsp. Mix chopped vegetables and chopped water chestnuts with meat, dressing and egg yolk until blended. Spoon onto centers of wonton wrappers, adding about 1 tsp. to each.
- Beat egg white lightly. Brush onto edges of wrappers; fold diagonally in half. Press edges together to seal. Bring opposite corners of long edge of each triangle together, overlapping corners; brush with remaining egg white to seal.
- Slice remaining onions; place in large saucepan. Add chicken broth, remaining mushrooms and remaining water chestnuts; bring to boil on medium heat. Carefully add wontons; simmer 4 min. or until wontons are done, stirring occasionally.

Nutrition Information

- Calories: 200
- Protein: 10 g
- Sugar: 0 g
- Saturated Fat: 2 g
- Total Carbohydrate: 0 g
- Total Fat: 6 g
- Fiber: 2 g
- Sodium: 660 mg
- Cholesterol: 45 mg

Chapter 3: Indian Recipes

***

54. Aloo Matar

Serving: 6 | Prep: 40mins | Cook: 10mins | Ready in: 50mins

Ingredients

- 1/4 cup KRAFT Zesty Lime Vinaigrette Dressing
- 1 onion, chopped
- 2 cloves garlic, minced
- 1 Tbsp. minced fresh ginger
- 2 tsp. garam masala
- 1 lb. baking potatoes (about 3), peeled, cut into 1-inch pieces
- 1 cup water
- 1-1/2 cups CLASSICO Spicy Red Pepper Pasta Sauce
- 1 cup frozen peas

Direction

- Heat dressing in medium saucepan on medium-high heat. Add onions; cook 3 to 4

min. or until crisp-tender, stirring frequently. Add garlic, ginger and garam masala; mix well. Cook and stir 1 min.
- Add potatoes and water, stir. Bring to boil. Cover; simmer on medium-low heat 10 min. Stir in pasta sauce. Return to boil; cover. Simmer on medium-low heat 10 to 15 min. or until potatoes are tender, stirring occasionally.
- Stir in peas; cook 1 min. or until heated through, stirring frequently.

Nutrition Information

- Calories: 120
- Total Fat: 2.5 g
- Fiber: 3 g
- Saturated Fat: 0 g
- Sugar: 0 g
- Protein: 4 g
- Sodium: 280 mg
- Total Carbohydrate: 0 g
- Cholesterol: 0 mg

55. Baked Butter Chicken

Serving: 8 | Prep: 10mins | Cook: 20mins | Ready in: 30mins

Ingredients

- 1/2 cup MIRACLE WHIP Dressing
- 1/4 cup tomato paste
- 2 Tbsp. KRAFT Classic CATALINA Dressing
- 1 tsp. ground cumin
- 1 tsp. garam masala
- 1/4 tsp. ground red pepper (cayenne)
- 8 small boneless skinless chicken breasts (2 lb.)
- 2 Tbsp. chopped fresh cilantro

Direction

- Heat oven to 350°F.
- Mix first 6 ingredients until blended. Pour over chicken in 13x9-inch baking dish sprayed with cooking spray; turn to evenly coat both sides of each breast. Cover.
- Bake 20 min. or until chicken is done (165°F).
- Sprinkle with cilantro.

Nutrition Information

- Calories: 190
- Saturated Fat: 1.5 g
- Sugar: 0 g
- Sodium: 370 mg
- Cholesterol: 70 mg
- Total Carbohydrate: 0 g
- Protein: 25 g
- Total Fat: 7 g
- Fiber: 0 g

56. Chicken Biryani Recipe

Serving: 0 | Prep: 10mins | Cook: 40mins | Ready in: 50mins

Ingredients

- 1 cup basmati rice, uncooked, rinsed
- 1 Tbsp. olive oil
- 1/2 tsp. cumin seed
- 1 onion, finely chopped
- 2 cloves garlic, minced
- 1 tsp. minced fresh ginger
- 1/2 lb. boneless skinless chicken breasts, cut into bite-size pieces
- 1 tsp. ground cumin
- 1-3/4 cups chicken broth
- 1/4 cup KRAFT Sun Dried Tomato Vinaigrette Dressing made with Extra Virgin Olive Oil
- 1 tsp. garam masala
- 1/2 tsp. ground turmeric
- 1/4 tsp. ground red pepper (cayenne)
- 1/2 cup plain nonfat Greek-style yogurt

Direction

- Place rice in medium bowl. Add enough cold water to cover rice. Let stand 10 min.
- Meanwhile, heat oil in large nonstick skillet on medium heat. Add cumin seed; cook and stir 30 sec. Stir in onions, garlic and ginger; cook 5 min. or until crisp-tender, stirring constantly. Add chicken and ground cumin; cook and stir 2 min.
- Drain rice. Add to chicken mixture with all remaining ingredients except yogurt; mix well. Bring to boil; cover. Simmer on low heat 22 to 24 min. or until rice is tender and liquid is absorbed. Serve topped with yogurt.

Nutrition Information

- Calories: 360
- Saturated Fat: 1.5 g
- Cholesterol: 35 mg
- Total Carbohydrate: 0 g
- Total Fat: 9 g
- Fiber: 2 g
- Sodium: 750 mg
- Protein: 22 g
- Sugar: 0 g

57. Chickpea And Tomato Stew

Serving: 0 | Prep: 35mins | Cook: |Ready in: 35mins

Ingredients

- 1/4 cup KRAFT Sun Dried Tomato Vinaigrette Dressing
- 1 small onion, chopped
- 4 cloves garlic, minced
- 1 tsp. ground cumin
- 1 tsp. garam masala
- 1 yellow pepper, cut into strips
- 1 can (28 oz.) diced tomatoes, drained
- 1 can (19 oz.) chickpeas (garbanzo beans), rinsed
- 2 cups loosely packed baby arugula

Direction

- Heat dressing in large saucepan on medium-high heat. Add onions and garlic; cook 5 min. or until crisp-tender, stirring frequently. Stir in seasonings; cook and stir 1 min. Add peppers; cook 3 min., stirring frequently.
- Stir in tomatoes and chickpeas; cover. Simmer on low heat 15 to 18 min. or until peppers are tender and mixture is thickened, stirring occasionally.
- Remove from heat. Stir in arugula.

Nutrition Information

- Calories: 190
- Cholesterol: 0 mg
- Protein: 9 g
- Total Carbohydrate: 0 g
- Fiber: 8 g
- Sugar: 0 g
- Total Fat: 4 g
- Saturated Fat: 0 g
- Sodium: 500 mg

58. Creamy Chicken Korma

Serving: 4 | Prep: 30mins | Cook: |Ready in: 30mins

Ingredients

- 1 lb. boneless skinless chicken breasts, cut into bite-size pieces
- 2 cloves garlic, minced
- 2 Tbsp. lemon juice
- 1 tsp. grated gingerroot
- 1 tsp. dried fenugreek leaves
- 1 tsp. ground coriander
- 1 tsp. ground cumin
- 1/2 tsp. ground red pepper (cayenne)
- 1/2 tsp. garam masala
- 1/2 tsp. ground fennel seed
- 1 Tbsp. oil
- 1/2 cup finely chopped onions

- 1/2 cup PHILADELPHIA Cream Cheese Spread
- 1/4 cup canned crushed tomatoes
- 1/4 cup water

Direction

- Combine first 10 ingredients; set aside. Heat oil in skillet on medium-high heat. Add onions; cook and stir 5 min. or just until crisp-tender. Add chicken mixture; cook 2 min. or until chicken is lightly browned, stirring occasionally.
- Add cream cheese spread, tomatoes and water; cook on medium heat 8 min. or until cream cheese is completely melted and chicken is done, stirring frequently.

Nutrition Information

- Calories: 260
- Fiber: 1 g
- Cholesterol: 85 mg
- Total Carbohydrate: 7 g
- Sugar: 2 g
- Total Fat: 14 g
- Saturated Fat: 6 g
- Sodium: 320 mg
- Protein: 27 g

59. Creamy Indian Butter Chicken

Serving: 4 | Prep: 30mins | Cook: | Ready in: 30mins

Ingredients

- 1 Tbsp. oil
- 1 onion, chopped
- 3 cloves garlic, minced
- 2 Tbsp. grated gingerroot
- 1 Tbsp. each garam masala and ground cumin
- 1 can (6 oz.) tomato paste
- 1/4 cup water
- 1 lb. boneless skinless chicken breasts, cut into bite-size pieces
- 1/2 cup PHILADELPHIA Cream Cheese Spread
- 1/4 cup milk
- 1/4 cup chopped fresh cilantro

Direction

- Heat oil in large skillet on medium heat. Add onions; cook 5 min. or until softened, stirring occasionally. Stir in garlic and ginger; cook 1 to 2 min. or until fragrant. Add garam masala and cumin; cook and stir 30 sec. Stir in tomato paste and water until blended.
- Add chicken to skillet; stir. Cover; simmer on medium-low heat 6 to 8 min. or until chicken is done, stirring occasionally.
- Add cream cheese spread and milk; cook and stir 2 to 3 min. or until cream cheese is completely melted and sauce is heated through. Sprinkle with cilantro.

Nutrition Information

- Calories: 310
- Fiber: 3 g
- Protein: 29 g
- Saturated Fat: 6 g
- Sugar: 4 g
- Cholesterol: 90 mg
- Sodium: 1130 mg
- Total Carbohydrate: 15 g
- Total Fat: 15 g

60. Creamy Indian Chutney Dip

Serving: 0 | Prep: 10mins | Cook: | Ready in: 10mins

Ingredients

- 2 Tbsp. lemon juice
- 2 Tbsp. water

- 1 tub (8 oz.) PHILADELPHIA Spicy Jalapeño Cream Cheese Spread
- 1 cup fresh cilantro
- 1/2 cup fresh mint
- 1/2 tsp. cumin seed

Direction

- Blend all ingredients in blender until smooth.

Nutrition Information

- Calories: 70
- Total Fat: 5 g
- Total Carbohydrate: 3 g
- Cholesterol: 20 mg
- Sodium: 170 mg
- Fiber: 1 g
- Sugar: 2 g
- Protein: 2 g
- Saturated Fat: 3 g

61. Curried Chicken And Rice

Serving: 4 | Prep: 30mins | Cook: | Ready in: 30mins

Ingredients

- 1 Tbsp. oil
- 1 lb. boneless skinless chicken breasts, cut into bite-size pieces
- 1 clove garlic, minced
- 1/2 cup fat-free reduced-sodium chicken broth
- 1/4 cup chopped chutney
- 3 Tbsp. raisins
- 1-1/2 tsp. curry powder
- 1 Tbsp. chopped fresh cilantro
- 1/4 tsp. pepper
- 3 cups hot cooked long-grain white rice
- 1/4 cup BAKER'S ANGEL FLAKE Coconut

Direction

- Heat oil in large nonstick skillet on medium-high heat. Add chicken and garlic; cook and stir 5 to 6 min. or until chicken is no longer pink.
- Add chicken broth, chutney, raisins and curry powder; mix well. Simmer on medium-low heat 5 min., stirring occasionally. Stir in cilantro and pepper.
- Place rice in large bowl. Add chicken mixture; mix lightly. Sprinkle with coconut.

Nutrition Information

- Calories: 450
- Saturated Fat: 3.5 g
- Sodium: 310 mg
- Total Carbohydrate: 0 g
- Protein: 28 g
- Cholesterol: 65 mg
- Total Fat: 9 g
- Fiber: 2 g
- Sugar: 0 g

62. Easy Coconut Curry

Serving: 0 | Prep: 20mins | Cook: | Ready in: 20mins

Ingredients

- 1/4 cup KRAFT Zesty Lime Vinaigrette Dressing, divided
- 1 Tbsp. each minced garlic and grated gingerroot
- 1 pkg. (16 oz.) frozen Asian mixed vegetables
- 1 can (13.5 oz.) lite coconut milk
- 1 Tbsp. red curry paste
- 2 tsp. lite soy sauce
- 2 cups instant brown rice, uncooked
- 1/4 cup PLANTERS Cashews, chopped

Direction

- Heat 2 Tbsp. dressing in large skillet on medium heat. Add garlic and ginger; cook and stir 1 min.

- Add remaining dressing and all remaining ingredients except rice and nuts; mix well. Cook 10 min. or until heated through, stirring frequently.
- Meanwhile, cook rice as directed on package, omitting salt.
- Serve rice topped with vegetable mixture and nuts.

Nutrition Information

- Calories: 300
- Saturated Fat: 5 g
- Total Carbohydrate: 0 g
- Cholesterol: 0 mg
- Sodium: 420 mg
- Fiber: 4 g
- Protein: 7 g
- Sugar: 0 g
- Total Fat: 11 g

63. India Inspired Chocolate Coconut Burfi

Serving: 18 | Prep: 15mins | Cook: 1hours | Ready in: 1hours15mins

Ingredients

- 1 cup plus 2 Tbsp. BAKER'S ANGEL FLAKE Unsweetened Coconut, divided
- 1 pkg. (8 oz.) PHILADELPHIA Cream Cheese, softened
- 1-1/2 pkg. (6 oz.) BAKER'S White Chocolate, melted
- 1 tsp. ground cardamom
- 2 oz. BAKER'S Semi-Sweet Chocolate, melted

Direction

- Cook 2 Tbsp. coconut in nonstick skillet on medium heat 2 min. or until crisp and lightly browned, stirring frequently.

- Beat cream cheese with mixer until creamy. Add remaining coconut, white chocolate and cardamom; mix well. Pat to 1/2-inch thickness on bottom of 8-inch square baking dish sprayed with cooking spray.
- Drizzle with semi-sweet chocolate; top with toasted coconut. Cut into squares. Refrigerate 1 hour or until firm.

Nutrition Information

- Calories: 160
- Saturated Fat: 8 g
- Cholesterol: 20 mg
- Sodium: 85 mg
- Total Fat: 12 g
- Sugar: 11 g
- Protein: 2 g
- Total Carbohydrate: 13 g
- Fiber: 1 g

64. Indian Chicken Curry

Serving: 4 | Prep: 40mins | Cook: | Ready in: 40mins

Ingredients

- 2 Tbsp. olive oil
- 1 lb. boneless skinless chicken breasts, cut into bite-size pieces
- 2 cloves garlic, minced
- 1 red pepper, cut into strips
- 1 cup frozen peas
- 2 green onions, sliced
- 1/2 cup MIRACLE WHIP Dressing
- 1 Tbsp. curry powder
- 3/4 cup fat-free reduced-sodium chicken broth
- 2 cups hot cooked long-grain white rice

Direction

- Heat oil in large skillet on medium heat. Add chicken and garlic; cook and stir 8 to 10 min. or until chicken is done. Remove from pan;

cover to keep warm. Add remaining oil, peppers, peas and green onions; cook and stir 3 to 4 min. or until peppers are tender.
- Mix dressing and curry powder until blended. Add to vegetable mixture in skillet; mix well. Stir in chicken. Add broth; cook 3 to 4 min. or until mixture is heated through and sauce is well blended.
- Serve over rice.

Nutrition Information

- Calories: 450
- Protein: 29 g
- Cholesterol: 75 mg
- Fiber: 4 g
- Sodium: 380 mg
- Saturated Fat: 3.5 g
- Sugar: 0 g
- Total Carbohydrate: 0 g
- Total Fat: 20 g

65. Indian Chicken Curry Recipe

Serving: 0 | Prep: 35mins | Cook: | Ready in: 35mins

Ingredients

- 1 sweet potato (8 oz.), peeled, cut into 3/4-inch pieces
- 1/3 cup KRAFT Zesty Lime Vinaigrette Dressing, divided
- 1 lb. boneless skinless chicken thighs, cut into bite-size pieces
- 1 small onion, finely chopped
- 1 Tbsp. grated fresh ginger
- 2 tsp. curry powder
- 1 Tbsp. flour
- 1 cup lite coconut milk
- 1 apple, chopped
- 1/4 cup PLANTERS Cashew Halves with Pieces
- 3 cups hot cooked basmati rice

Direction

- Cook potatoes in pan of boiling water 5 min.; drain. Rinse under cold water to cool.
- Heat 1 Tbsp. dressing in large skillet on medium-high heat. Add chicken; cook and stir 4 min. or until lightly browned. Remove from skillet; cover to keep warm.
- Add 2 Tbsp. of the remaining dressing, onions, ginger, curry powder and potatoes to skillet; cook and stir 5 min. or until vegetables are tender.
- Whisk flour and remaining dressing in medium bowl until blended. Gradually whisk in coconut milk. Add to potato mixture in skillet along with the apples and chicken; stir. Simmer on medium heat 3 to 5 min. or until chicken is done and sauce is thickened, stirring occasionally. Sprinkle with nuts. Serve with rice.

Nutrition Information

- Calories: 360
- Fiber: 3 g
- Total Fat: 13 g
- Saturated Fat: 4 g
- Protein: 18 g
- Sodium: 220 mg
- Cholesterol: 65 mg
- Total Carbohydrate: 0 g
- Sugar: 0 g

66. Indian Chicken Tikka Masala

Serving: 6 | Prep: 30mins | Cook: | Ready in: 30mins

Ingredients

- 1-1/2 lb. boneless skinless chicken breasts, cut into bite-size pieces
- 2 Tbsp. fresh lemon juice, divided

- 1 tsp. each garam masala, ground coriander, ground cumin and ground red pepper (cayenne), divided
- 1 cup canned crushed tomatoes
- 1/3 cup MIRACLE WHIP Dressing
- 1/4 cup water
- 1 Tbsp. oil
- 1/2 cup chopped onions
- 2 cloves garlic, minced
- 1 tsp. minced fresh ginger
- 1/2 tsp. cumin seed
- 2 Tbsp. chopped fresh cilantro

Direction

- Combine chicken, 1 Tbsp. lemon juice and 1/2 tsp. of each of the dry seasonings; set aside. Mix tomatoes, dressing, water and remaining dry seasonings in separate bowl.
- Heat oil in large skillet on medium heat. Add onions, garlic, ginger and cumin seed; cook and stir 3 min. or until onions are crisp-tender. Add chicken mixture; cook 2 min. or until chicken is lightly browned, stirring occasionally.
- Add tomato mixture; cook 8 min. or until sauce is thickened and chicken is done, stirring frequently. Remove from heat.
- Stir in cilantro and remaining lemon juice.

Nutrition Information

- Calories: 210
- Total Carbohydrate: 0 g
- Total Fat: 8 g
- Cholesterol: 70 mg
- Fiber: 1 g
- Saturated Fat: 1.5 g
- Sodium: 380 mg
- Sugar: 0 g
- Protein: 25 g

67. Indian Peanut Butter Nankhatai Cookies

Serving: 30 | Prep: 15mins | Cook: 30mins | Ready in: 45mins

Ingredients

- 1 cup creamy peanut butter
- 1/2 cup sugar
- 1 cup flour
- 1/2 cup dried cranberries
- 2 tsp. ground cardamom
- 1/2 tsp. CALUMET Baking Powder
- 1/4 cup milk

Direction

- Heat oven to 300°F.
- Beat peanut butter and sugar in large bowl with mixer until light and fluffy. Combine flour, cranberries, cardamom and baking powder. Add to peanut butter mixture along with milk; beat just until blended. (Mixture will be slightly crumbly.)
- Roll into 30 balls, using about 1 Tbsp. dough for each. Place, 1 inch apart, on baking sheets. Flatten slightly.
- Bake 12 to 15 min. or until lightly browned. Cool on baking sheets 3 min. Remove to wire racks; cool completely.

Nutrition Information

- Calories: 90
- Total Fat: 4.5 g
- Saturated Fat: 1 g
- Total Carbohydrate: 10 g
- Sodium: 50 mg
- Protein: 3 g
- Fiber: 1 g
- Sugar: 6 g
- Cholesterol: 0 mg

68. Indian Vegetarian Dal Biryani

Serving: 0 | Prep: 20mins | Cook: 42mins | Ready in: 1hours2mins

Ingredients

- 1-1/4 qt. (5 cups) water, divided
- 1 cup dry lentils, uncooked
- 1 cup basmati rice, uncooked
- 1/4 cup MIRACLE WHIP Dressing
- 1 tsp. garam masala
- 1 tsp. ground cumin
- 1 tsp. ground coriander
- 1 tsp. dried fenugreek leaves
- 1/2 tsp. ground red pepper (cayenne)
- 1/2 tsp. ground turmeric
- 2 plum tomatoes, finely chopped
- 1 Tbsp. oil
- 1 onion, finely chopped
- 2 cloves garlic, minced
- 1 Tbsp. minced fresh ginger
- 1/2 tsp. cumin seed

Direction

- Bring 1 qt. (4 cups) water to boil in large saucepan. Meanwhile, combine lentils and rice in medium bowl. Add enough cold water to completely cover lentil mixture. Let stand 10 min.
- Drain lentil mixture. Add to boiling water; stir. Return to boil; simmer on medium-low heat 10 to 12 min. or just until lentils and rice are tender. Drain.
- Mix MIRACLE WHIP, seasonings and remaining 1 cup water in medium bowl until blended. Stir in tomatoes.
- Heat oil in large skillet on medium heat. Add onions, garlic, ginger and cumin; cook and stir 4 min. or until onions are crisp-tender. Stir in MIRACLE WHIP mixture and lentil mixture; cover. Simmer on medium-low heat 30 min. or until liquid is absorbed. Remove from heat. Let stand 10 min. Fluff with fork.

Nutrition Information

- Calories: 440
- Saturated Fat: 1 g
- Total Fat: 8 g
- Cholesterol: 5 mg
- Protein: 18 g
- Total Carbohydrate: 0 g
- Sodium: 310 mg
- Fiber: 17 g
- Sugar: 0 g

69. Indian Style Chicken Koftas

Serving: 4 | Prep: 15mins | Cook: 25mins | Ready in: 40mins

Ingredients

- 2 green chiles
- 1 piece gingerroot (1 inch), peeled
- 1/4 cup fresh mint
- 1/4 cup fresh cilantro
- 1 lb. lean ground chicken
- 1 egg
- 1-1/2 tsp. garam masala, divided
- 1 tsp. ground cumin
- 1 cup water
- 1 Tbsp. cornstarch
- 1/4 cup KRAFT Classic CATALINA Dressing
- 2 Tbsp. lite soy sauce
- 1/2 tsp. crushed red pepper
- 2 green onions, chopped
- 2 Tbsp. chopped fresh cilantro

Direction

- Heat oven to 400°F.
- Process first 4 ingredients in food processor until blended. Add chicken, egg, 1 tsp. garam masala and cumin; process just until blended. Shape into 24 (1-inch) balls. Place in 13x9-inch baking dish sprayed with cooking spray.
- Bake 15 min. Meanwhile, gradually stir water into cornstarch in small bowl. Add remaining garam masala, dressing, soy sauce and crushed pepper; mix well.

- Pour sauce over meatballs. Bake 10 min. or until sauce is thickened and meatballs are done (165°F). Stir in onions and chopped cilantro.

Nutrition Information

- Calories: 250
- Sodium: 870 mg
- Total Fat: 15 g
- Fiber: 1 g
- Sugar: 7 g
- Protein: 22 g
- Cholesterol: 125 mg
- Total Carbohydrate: 12 g
- Saturated Fat: 2.5 g

70. Indian Style Grilled Chicken Tikka

Serving: 6 | Prep: 30mins | Cook: 30mins | Ready in: 1hours

Ingredients

- 1/2 cup MIRACLE WHIP Dressing
- 2 Tbsp. lemon juice
- 1 tsp. each dried fenugreek leaves, garam masala, ground coriander and ground cumin
- 1 tsp. minced fresh ginger
- 1/4 tsp. chili powder
- 1-1/2 lb. boneless skinless chicken breasts, cut into 1-inch pieces

Direction

- Mix all ingredients except chicken until blended; pour over chicken in shallow dish. Stir to evenly coat chicken. Refrigerate 30 min. to marinate.
- Heat grill to medium heat. Drain chicken; discard marinade. Thread chicken onto skewers.
- Grill 20 min. or until chicken is done, turning occasionally.

Nutrition Information

- Calories: 160
- Total Fat: 5 g
- Sodium: 190 mg
- Sugar: 0 g
- Protein: 24 g
- Total Carbohydrate: 0 g
- Cholesterol: 70 mg
- Saturated Fat: 1 g
- Fiber: 0 g

71. Indian Style Sheer Khurma Dessert

Serving: 0 | Prep: 20mins | Cook: 20mins | Ready in: 40mins

Ingredients

- 17 KRAFT Caramels
- 2 cups 2% milk
- 1 can (12 oz.) evaporated milk
- 1/2 cup PLANTERS Trail Mix Fruit & Nut Mix, chopped
- 1/2 cup 1-inch lengths angel hair pasta, uncooked
- 1/4 tsp. saffron threads
- 1 tsp. ground cardamom

Direction

- Cook and stir first 3 ingredients in large saucepan on high heat 10 min. or until caramels are completely melted and sauce is well blended.
- Add next 3 ingredients; stir. Cover; simmer on medium-low heat 20 min. or until pasta is tender. Remove from heat.
- Stir in cardamom. Serve warm.

Nutrition Information

- Calories: 220
- Total Carbohydrate: 29 g
- Fiber: 1 g
- Protein: 8 g
- Sodium: 135 mg
- Sugar: 23 g
- Saturated Fat: 4.5 g
- Cholesterol: 20 mg
- Total Fat: 9 g

72. Indian Style Stir Fried Tandoori Shrimp

Serving: 6 | Prep: 20mins | Cook: | Ready in: 20mins

Ingredients

- 1 lb. uncooked deveined peeled medium shrimp
- 1/4 cup KRAFT Cucumber Ranch Dressing
- 2 Tbsp. lemon juice
- 2 cloves garlic, minced
- 1 Tbsp. minced gingerroot
- 1 tsp. dried fenugreek leaves
- 1 tsp. garam masala
- 1 tsp. ground coriander
- 1 tsp. ground cumin
- 1/2 tsp. ground red pepper (cayenne)
- 1 Tbsp. oil
- 2 Tbsp. chopped fresh cilantro
- 2 Tbsp. chopped fresh mint

Direction

- Toss shrimp with dressing, lemon juice, garlic, ginger and dry seasonings.
- Heat oil in large skillet on medium-high heat. Add shrimp mixture; cook and stir 5 min. or until shrimp turn pink.
- Remove from heat. Stir in remaining ingredients.

Nutrition Information

- Calories: 140
- Total Fat: 7 g
- Total Carbohydrate: 3 g
- Saturated Fat: 1 g
- Protein: 14 g
- Fiber: 1 g
- Cholesterol: 125 mg
- Sodium: 770 mg
- Sugar: 1 g

73. Madras Curry Chicken

Serving: 0 | Prep: 15mins | Cook: 20mins | Ready in: 35mins

Ingredients

- 1 Tbsp. butter or margarine
- 1/2 cup chopped green peppers
- 1/2 cup chopped onions
- 1 clove garlic, minced
- 2 tsp. curry powder
- 1-1/2 lb. boneless skinless chicken breasts, cut into bite-size pieces
- 1 can (14-1/2 oz.) diced tomatoes, drained
- 1 tsp. lemon juice
- 1/2 tsp. dried thyme leaves
- 1/8 tsp. black pepper
- 1/2 lb. (8 oz.) VELVEETA, cut into 1/2-inch cubes
- 3 cups cooked long-grain white rice

Direction

- Melt butter in large saucepan on medium heat. Add green peppers, onions, garlic and curry powder; cook and stir until vegetables are crisp-tender. Add chicken; cook and stir 5 min. or until no longer pink.
- Stir in tomatoes, lemon juice, thyme and black pepper; simmer on low heat 5 min. or until chicken is done, stirring occasionally.

- Add VELVEETA; cook until melted, stirring frequently. Serve over rice.

Nutrition Information

- Calories: 330
- Protein: 26 g
- Sodium: 640 mg
- Sugar: 4 g
- Total Fat: 10 g
- Total Carbohydrate: 30 g
- Cholesterol: 80 mg
- Saturated Fat: 5 g
- Fiber: 2 g

74. Mango Chutney Curry Dip

Serving: 0 | Prep: 10mins | Cook: | Ready in: 10mins

Ingredients

- 1 mango, chopped, divided
- 1 pkg. (8 oz.) PHILADELPHIA Cream Cheese, cubed, softened
- 1 tsp. curry powder
- 1/4 cup chopped red peppers
- 1/4 cup chopped red onions
- 1/4 cup golden raisins
- 1/4 cup chopped fresh cilantro

Direction

- Process 1 cup mangos, cream cheese and curry powder in food processor until smooth; spread onto bottom of pie plate.
- Combine remaining ingredients; spread over cream cheese mixture.

Nutrition Information

- Calories: 60
- Protein: 1 g
- Sodium: 50 mg
- Total Carbohydrate: 4 g
- Saturated Fat: 2.5 g
- Cholesterol: 15 mg
- Fiber: 0 g
- Total Fat: 4.5 g
- Sugar: 4 g

75. One Pot Curry & Rice

Serving: 0 | Prep: 20mins | Cook: 15mins | Ready in: 35mins

Ingredients

- 1/2 cup KRAFT Classic CATALINA Dressing
- 1 to 2 Tbsp. curry powder
- 1 lb. boneless skinless chicken breasts, cut into strips
- 2 stalks celery, chopped (about 1 cup)
- 2 large carrots, thinly sliced (about 1 cup)
- 4 green onions, sliced
- 1 can (14-1/2 oz.) chicken broth
- 1-1/2 cups instant white rice, uncooked
- 1/2 cup chopped dried apricots
- 1/2 cup PLANTERS Cashews
- 2 tsp. ground ginger

Direction

- Mix dressing and curry powder; pour over chicken. Cover and refrigerate 10 minutes.
- Pour chicken mixture into large skillet. Add celery, carrots and onions; mix well. Cook on medium-high heat 2 minutes, stirring occasionally. Stir in chicken broth. Bring to boil. Cover skillet. Reduce heat to medium-low; simmer 5 minutes.
- Add rice, apricots, cashews and ginger; mix well. Remove from heat. Let stand, covered, 5 minutes. Stir before serving.

Nutrition Information

- Calories: 530
- Fiber: 5 g

- Sugar: 0 g
- Saturated Fat: 3.5 g
- Sodium: 930 mg
- Protein: 33 g
- Total Carbohydrate: 0 g
- Total Fat: 18 g
- Cholesterol: 65 mg

76. Sri Lankan Fish Curry

Serving: 6 | Prep: 35mins | Cook: 10mins | Ready in: 45mins

Ingredients

- 1/2 cup water
- 1 Tbsp. seedless tamarind (about 1-inch piece)
- 1/2 cup canned coconut milk
- 1/4 cup KRAFT Sun Dried Tomato Vinaigrette Dressing
- 1/2 tsp. ground red pepper (cayenne)
- 1/2 tsp. ground turmeric
- 1 Tbsp. oil
- 1 onion, finely chopped
- 2 fresh green chiles, sliced
- 20 fresh curry leaves
- 2 cloves garlic, minced
- 1 Tbsp. minced gingerroot
- 1/2 tsp. fennel seed
- 1/2 tsp. black mustard seed
- 2 tomatoes, chopped
- 1-1/2 lb. halibut fillet, cut into 2-inch chunks

Direction

- Microwave water and tamarind in medium microwaveable bowl on HIGH 1 min. Mash with fork; let stand 5 min. Strain tamarind through fine-mesh sieve over bowl; firmly press strained tamarind to remove all liquid. Reserve strained liquid in bowl; discard tamarind in sieve. Add coconut milk, dressing, red pepper and turmeric to reserved liquid; mix well.
- Heat oil in large skillet on medium heat. Add next 7 ingredients; cook and stir 5 min. or until onions are crisp-tender. Stir in tomatoes; cook and stir 5 min. Add coconut milk mixture; stir. Bring to boil. Add fish; cover. Simmer on medium-low heat 10 min. or until fish flakes easily with fork.
- Transfer fish to platter; top with sauce.

Nutrition Information

- Calories: 200
- Sugar: 5 g
- Protein: 22 g
- Cholesterol: 55 mg
- Sodium: 200 mg
- Total Fat: 9 g
- Fiber: 1 g
- Saturated Fat: 4 g
- Total Carbohydrate: 8 g

77. Tandoori Chicken

Serving: 4 | Prep: 15mins | Cook: 2hours24mins | Ready in: 2hours39mins

Ingredients

- 1/4 cup BULL'S-EYE Original Barbecue Sauce
- 1/4 cup plain nonfat Greek-style yogurt
- 2 Tbsp. lemon juice
- 1 Tbsp. oil
- 2 cloves garlic, minced
- 1 tsp. ground coriander
- 1 tsp. ground cumin
- 1 tsp. dried fenugreek leaves
- 1 tsp. garam masala
- 1 tsp. minced gingerroot
- 1/4 tsp. chili powder
- 1-1/2 lb. chicken drumsticks, skin removed

Direction

- Mix all ingredients except chicken. Reserve 1/4 of the sauce. Pour remaining over chicken in shallow dish; turn to coat both sides of each drumstick. Refrigerate 2 hours to marinate.
- Heat grill to medium-high heat. Remove chicken from marinade; discard marinade. Grill chicken 24 min. or until done (165ºF), turning and brushing occasionally with reserved sauce.

Nutrition Information

- Calories: 210
- Cholesterol: 120 mg
- Saturated Fat: 1.5 g
- Sugar: 0 g
- Total Carbohydrate: 0 g
- Protein: 24 g
- Total Fat: 9 g
- Fiber: 0 g
- Sodium: 250 mg

Chapter 4: Southern Recipes

***

78. Baking Powder Biscuits

Serving: 0 | Prep: 20mins | Cook: 10mins | Ready in: 30mins

Ingredients

- 1-3/4 cups flour
- 1 Tbsp. CALUMET Baking Powder
- 1/2 tsp. salt
- 1/3 cup margarine
- 3/4 cup milk

Direction

- Preheat oven to 450°F. Mix flour, baking powder and salt in large bowl. Cut in margarine until mixture resembles coarse crumbs. Add milk; stir with fork until soft dough forms.
- Place on lightly floured surface; knead 20 times or until smooth. Pat or roll lightly until dough is 1/2-inch thick. Cut with floured 2-inch cookie cutter to make 16 biscuits, rerolling dough scraps as necessary. Place on ungreased baking sheet.
- Bake 10 minutes or until golden brown.

Nutrition Information

- Calories: 180
- Total Carbohydrate: 0 g
- Cholesterol: 0 mg
- Fiber: 0.7383 g
- Sodium: 330 mg
- Protein: 4 g
- Sugar: 0 g
- Total Fat: 8 g
- Saturated Fat: 2 g

79. Bananas Foster Cheesecake Squares

Serving: 16 | Prep: 20mins | Cook: 4hours30mins | Ready in: 4hours50mins

Ingredients

- 2 cups finely crushed vanilla wafers
- 1/2 cup chopped PLANTERS Pecans
- 1/4 cup butter or margarine, melted
- 3/4 cup packed brown sugar, divided
- 3 pkg. (8 oz. each) PHILADELPHIA Cream Cheese, softened
- 2 tsp. rum extract
- 3 eggs

- 1/2 cup mashed fully ripe bananas (about 1 large)
- 2 bananas
- 2 tsp. lemon juice
- 25 KRAFT Caramels
- 2 Tbsp. milk
- 1/2 cup PLANTERS Pecan Halves

Direction

- Heat oven to 350°F.
- Combine wafer crumbs, chopped nuts, butter and 1/4 cup sugar; press onto bottom of 13x9-inch pan sprayed with cooking spray.
- Beat cream cheese, rum extract and remaining sugar in large bowl with mixer until blended. Add eggs, one at a time, mixing on low speed after each just until blended. Stir in mashed bananas; pour over crust.
- Bake 30 min. or until center is almost set. Cool. Refrigerate 3 hours.
- Slice remaining bananas; toss with lemon juice. Spoon over cheesecake. Microwave caramels and milk in microwaveable bowl on HIGH 2 min.; stir until caramels are completely melted and sauce is well blended. Drizzle over cheesecake; top with pecan halves.

Nutrition Information

- Calories: 410
- Total Fat: 28 g
- Sodium: 290 mg
- Total Carbohydrate: 37 g
- Saturated Fat: 13 g
- Sugar: 26 g
- Fiber: 2 g
- Cholesterol: 90 mg
- Protein: 6 g

80. Blackened Tilapia Po' Boy

Serving: 0 | Prep: 20mins | Cook: | Ready in: 20mins

Ingredients

- 5 tilapia fillets (1-1/4 lb.)
- 3 Tbsp. Cajun seasoning, divided
- 1/3 cup KRAFT Avocado Oil Mayonnaise
- 1 baguette (20 inch), partially split, cut crosswise into 5 pieces
- 2 plum tomatoes, each cut into 5 slices
- 2-1/2 cups shredded romaine lettuce

Direction

- Season fish with 2 Tbsp. seasoning. Mix remaining seasoning and mayo.
- Heat large nonstick skillet on medium-high heat. Add fish; cook 5 min. on each side or until fish flakes easily with fork. Meanwhile, spread mayo mixture onto cut sides of bread.
- Fill bread with fish, tomatoes and lettuce.

Nutrition Information

- Calories: 220
- Protein: 25 g
- Sugar: 1 g
- Fiber: 1 g
- Cholesterol: 60 mg
- Total Fat: 7 g
- Saturated Fat: 1.5 g
- Total Carbohydrate: 13 g
- Sodium: 1190 mg

81. Buttermilk Biscuits

Serving: 0 | Prep: 20mins | Cook: 12mins | Ready in: 32mins

Ingredients

- 2 cups flour
- 4 tsp. CALUMET Baking Powder
- 1/2 tsp. salt
- 1/2 tsp. cream of tartar
- 1/4 tsp. baking soda
- 1/3 cup shortening

- 1 cup buttermilk
- 2 Tbsp. butter or margarine, melted, divided

Direction

- Heat oven to 450°F.
- Mix flour, baking powder, salt, cream of tartar and baking soda in large bowl until well blended. Cut in shortening until mixture resembles coarse crumbs. Add buttermilk; stir with fork until mixture forms a soft dough.
- Place on lightly floured surface; knead 20 times or until smooth. Pat or roll out dough to 1/2-inch-thickness. Cut into circles with floured 2-inch cookie cutter. Place on ungreased baking sheet. Brush with half of the butter.
- Bake 12 minutes or until golden brown. Brush with remaining butter.

Nutrition Information

- Calories: 100
- Fiber: 0 g
- Total Fat: 5 g
- Sugar: 0.6895 g
- Total Carbohydrate: 11 g
- Saturated Fat: 2 g
- Sodium: 220 mg
- Cholesterol: 3.8778 mg
- Protein: 2 g

82. Carolina Style BBQ Pulled Pork Sliders

Serving: 0 | Prep: | Cook: | Ready in:

Ingredients

- 1 pork shoulder (3 lb.), trimmed of fat
- 1 tsp. garlic powder
- 1 bottle (12 oz.) beer
- 1 bottle (18.6 oz.) HEINZ BBQ Sauce Carolina Tangy Vinegar Style, divided
- 2 Tbsp. HEINZ Yellow Mustard
- 2 Tbsp. sugar
- 1/4 cup HEINZ Apple Cider Vinegar
- 1 pkg. (5 oz.) coleslaw blend (cabbage slaw mix)
- 12 slider buns (2 inch), split

Direction

- Season meat with garlic powder; place in slow cooker. Add beer and 1/2 cup barbecue sauce; cover with lid. Cook on LOW 8 to 10 hours (or on HIGH 4 to 5 hours). Meanwhile, mix mustard, sugar and vinegar until blended. Add to coleslaw blend in medium bowl; mix lightly. Refrigerate until ready to serve.
- Transfer meat to cutting board. Discard all but 1/4 cup sauce from slow cooker. Pull meat into shreds with 2 forks. Add to reserved sauce in slow cooker; stir in remaining barbecue sauce.
- Fill rolls with meat mixture and coleslaw just before serving.

Nutrition Information

- Calories: 0 g
- Protein: 0 g
- Sodium: 0 g
- Fiber: 0 g
- Saturated Fat: 0 g
- Total Fat: 0 g
- Cholesterol: 0 g
- Total Carbohydrate: 0 g
- Sugar: 0 g

83. Chicken 'n Waffle Tacos

Serving: 4 | Prep: 25mins | Cook: | Ready in: 25mins

Ingredients

- 1 lb. boneless skinless chicken breasts, cut lengthwise into 16 strips

- 1 pkt. SHAKE 'N BAKE Extra Crispy Seasoned Coating Mix
- 8 round frozen waffles, thawed
- 1/3 cup maple-flavored or pancake syrup
- 2 Tbsp. KRAFT Original Barbecue Sauce
- 1/2 tsp. Sriracha sauce (hot chili sauce)
- 1 green onion, thinly sliced

Direction

- Heat oven to 400°F.
- Coat chicken with coating mix as directed on package; place on baking sheet. Bake 12 to 15 min. or until done.
- Meanwhile, spray both sides of waffles with cooking spray. Gently fold each in half; secure with wooden toothpick. Place on separate baking sheet. Add to oven to bake with chicken for the last 8 min. Mix syrup, barbecue sauce and Sriracha sauce until blended.
- Remove toothpicks from waffles. Place chicken strips in waffle shells; top with syrup mixture and onions.

Nutrition Information

- Calories: 460
- Sodium: 1280 mg
- Sugar: 21 g
- Total Fat: 10 g
- Saturated Fat: 2 g
- Cholesterol: 90 mg
- Protein: 30 g
- Total Carbohydrate: 62 g
- Fiber: 2 g

84. Cookie Crumb Topped Apple Crisp

Serving: 0 | Prep: 20mins | Cook: 35mins | Ready in: 55mins

Ingredients

- 4 large Granny Smith apples (2 lb.), peeled, thinly sliced
- 1/2 cup packed brown sugar, divided
- 2 tsp. ground cinnamon, divided
- 1/3 cup old-fashioned or quick-cooking oats
- 1/4 cup cold margarine
- 25 reduced-fat vanilla wafers, crushed
- 1-1/2 cups thawed COOL WHIP LITE Whipped Topping

Direction

- Heat oven to 350°F.
- Toss apples with 1/4 cup sugar and 1 tsp. cinnamon; place in 8- or 9-inch square baking dish.
- Combine oats, remaining sugar and cinnamon in medium bowl. Cut in margarine with pastry blender or 2 knives until mixture resembles coarse crumbs. Stir in wafer crumbs; sprinkle over apples.
- Bake 30 to 35 min. or until apples are tender. Serve topped with COOL WHIP.

Nutrition Information

- Calories: 160
- Protein: 1 g
- Sodium: 80 mg
- Cholesterol: 0 mg
- Fiber: 1 g
- Total Carbohydrate: 0 g
- Sugar: 0 g
- Saturated Fat: 2 g
- Total Fat: 6 g

85. Family Reunion Macaroni Salad

Serving: 0 | Prep: 20mins | Cook: | Ready in: 20mins

Ingredients

- 2 pkg. (14 oz. each) KRAFT Deluxe Macaroni & Cheese Dinner

- 1 cup MIRACLE WHIP Dressing
- 1/2 cup milk
- 1/2 cup finely chopped celery
- 1 small red pepper, finely chopped
- 4 hard-cooked eggs, chopped
- 8 green onions, sliced

Direction

- Prepare Dinners as directed on package.
- Add remaining ingredients; mix lightly.

Nutrition Information

- Calories: 250
- Total Fat: 12 g
- Cholesterol: 65 mg
- Fiber: 0.9027 g
- Total Carbohydrate: 26 g
- Sugar: 5 g
- Protein: 8 g
- Saturated Fat: 2.5 g
- Sodium: 650 mg

86. Iyanla's Divine Mac & Cheese

Serving: 0 | Prep: 15mins | Cook: 15mins | Ready in: 30mins

Ingredients

- 1 pkg. (14 oz.) KRAFT Deluxe Macaroni & Cheese Dinner
- 1/2 cup cubed KRAFT Extra Sharp Cheddar Cheese (1/2 inch)
- 1/4 cup KRAFT Shredded Cheddar Cheese
- 1/4 cup KRAFT Shredded Low-Moisture Part-Skim Mozzarella Cheese
- 1 egg
- 1/2 cup milk
- 1/4 tsp. black pepper

Direction

- Preheat oven to 375°F. Prepare Dinner as directed on package. Meanwhile, combine cubed and shredded cheeses; set aside. Beat egg, milk and pepper with wire whisk until well blended.
- Spoon half of the Dinner into greased 2-qt. casserole dish; cover with half of the cheese mixture. Repeat layers. Drizzle evenly with egg mixture.
- Bake 15 min. or until center is set and Dinner mixture is heated through.

Nutrition Information

- Calories: 460
- Cholesterol: 95 mg
- Saturated Fat: 9 g
- Protein: 21 g
- Sugar: 0 g
- Total Carbohydrate: 0 g
- Fiber: 2 g
- Sodium: 1180 mg
- Total Fat: 22 g

87. Mac And Cheese Jalapeño Bites

Serving: 30 | Prep: 30mins | Cook: 20mins | Ready in: 50mins

Ingredients

- 1 pkg. (14 oz.) KRAFT Deluxe Macaroni & Cheese Dinner
- 48 RITZ Crackers, finely crushed (about 2 cups), divided
- 1 egg, beaten
- 4 slices OSCAR MAYER Bacon, cooked, crumbled
- 2 tsp. chopped drained pickled jalapeño nacho slices
- 4 oz. (1/4 of 16-oz. pkg.) VELVEETA, cut into 30 cubes
- vegetable oil

Direction

- Prepare Dinner in large saucepan as directed on package. Stir in 1 cup cracker crumbs, egg, bacon and jalapeno peppers until blended. Cool 20 min.
- Shape into 30 balls, using scant 1/4 cup macaroni mixture for each ball. Insert 1 VELVEETA cube into center of each ball, completely enclosing VELVEETA cube. Roll in remaining cracker crumbs until evenly coated. Place in single layer on waxed paper-covered baking sheet.
- Heat oil to 375ºF in deep fryer. Add balls, a few at a time; cook 2 min. or until golden brown. Drain well. Serve warm.

Nutrition Information

- Calories: 130
- Cholesterol: 15 mg
- Saturated Fat: 2 g
- Sodium: 250 mg
- Fiber: 0 g
- Sugar: 1 g
- Protein: 3 g
- Total Carbohydrate: 10 g
- Total Fat: 9 g

88. Memphis Style Muffuletta

Serving: 8 | Prep: 20mins | Cook: 1hours | Ready in: 1hours20mins

Ingredients

- 1/2 cup KRAFT Mayo with Olive Oil Reduced Fat Mayonnaise
- 1/4 cup KRAFT Zesty Italian Dressing
- 2 stalks celery, chopped
- 1/2 cup chopped drained canned artichoke hearts
- 1/2 cup chopped black olives
- 1/4 cup chopped pimento-stuffed green olives
- 1/8 tsp. ground black pepper
- 1 round Italian bread loaf (10 inch), cut horizontally in half
- 6 slices each OSCAR MAYER Deli Fresh Bold Cajun Style Chicken Breast, Deli Fresh Slow Roasted Roast Beef, Smoked Ham and Smoked Turkey Breast
- 4 KRAFT Singles

Direction

- Mix mayo and dressing in medium bowl; stir in celery, artichokes, olives and pepper.
- Spread half the olive mixture onto bottom half of bread; top with meat, Singles and remaining olive mixture. Cover with top of bread.
- Wrap tightly in plastic wrap. Refrigerate 1 hour.

Nutrition Information

- Calories: 330
- Protein: 13 g
- Sugar: 5 g
- Cholesterol: 25 mg
- Total Carbohydrate: 40 g
- Fiber: 3 g
- Saturated Fat: 3 g
- Sodium: 1210 mg
- Total Fat: 12 g

89. Mini Memphis Style BBQ Burgers

Serving: 8 | Prep: 20mins | Cook: | Ready in: 20mins

Ingredients

- 1 lb. lean ground beef
- 2 Tbsp. finely chopped red onions
- 4 KRAFT Singles, halved
- 8 slider buns, toasted
- 1/2 cup coleslaw

- 4 slices OSCAR MAYER Bacon, cooked, cut in half
- 1/3 cup BULL'S-EYE Memphis Style Barbecue Sauce

Direction

- Heat grill to medium-high heat.
- Mix meat and onions just until blended; shape into 8 (1/2-inch-thick) patties.
- Grill 3 min. on each side or until done (160°F), topping with Singles halves for the last minute.
- Fill buns with cheeseburgers and remaining ingredients.

Nutrition Information

- Calories: 230
- Sugar: 0 g
- Saturated Fat: 3.5 g
- Cholesterol: 40 mg
- Fiber: 0 g
- Total Fat: 9 g
- Total Carbohydrate: 0 g
- Protein: 14 g
- Sodium: 470 mg

90. Oven Fried Catfish Recipe

Serving: 8 | Prep: 10mins | Cook: 30mins | Ready in: 40mins

Ingredients

- 1/2 cup MIRACLE WHIP Dressing
- 2 tsp. Creole seasoning
- 1 cup crushed corn flakes
- 1/2 cup KRAFT Grated Parmesan Cheese
- 4 large catfish fillets (2 lb.)

Direction

- Heat oven to 375°F.
- Cover rimmed baking sheet with cooking spray. Mix dressing and seasoning in shallow dish until blended. Combine corn flake crumbs and cheese in separate shallow dish.
- Dip fish fillets, 1 at a time, into dressing mixture, then corn flake crumb mixture, turning to evenly coat both sides of each fillet with each mixture. Place on prepared baking sheet.
- Bake 25 to 30 min. or until fish flakes easily with fork.

Nutrition Information

- Calories: 200
- Saturated Fat: 2.5 g
- Total Fat: 10 g
- Cholesterol: 65 mg
- Fiber: 0 g
- Sodium: 430 mg
- Sugar: 0 g
- Protein: 19 g
- Total Carbohydrate: 0 g

91. Peach Cobbler Recipe

Serving: 9 | Prep: 25mins | Cook: 30mins | Ready in: 55mins

Ingredients

- 8 fresh peaches, sliced (about 5 cups)
- 1/3 cup maple-flavored or pancake syrup
- 1/4 cup packed brown sugar
- 2 Tbsp. MINUTE Tapioca
- 1 Tbsp. lemon juice
- 1/2 tsp. ground cinnamon
- 1/4 tsp. ground nutmeg
- 1 cup all-purpose baking mix
- 2 Tbsp. granulated sugar
- 1/4 cup milk

Direction

- Heat oven to 375°F.
- Toss peaches with next 6 ingredients in large saucepan. Bring to boil on medium heat, stirring occasionally. Pour into 9-inch square baking dish.
- Stir baking mix, granulated sugar and milk in medium bowl until mixture forms soft dough. Drop by heaping tablespoonfuls onto hot fruit mixture.
- Bake 28 to 30 min. or until biscuits are golden brown.

Nutrition Information

- Calories: 150
- Total Carbohydrate: 0 g
- Total Fat: 0.5 g
- Sodium: 150 mg
- Sugar: 0 g
- Protein: 3 g
- Fiber: 2 g
- Saturated Fat: 0 g
- Cholesterol: 0 mg

92. Praline Sweet Potatoes

Serving: 8 | Prep: 30mins | Cook: 30mins | Ready in: 1hours

Ingredients

- 2 lb. sweet potato es (about 7), cooked, peeled
- 1/2 cup MIRACLE WHIP Dressing
- 1/2 cup packed brown sugar, divided
- 1 tsp. ground ginger
- 1/4 tsp. orange zest
- 1/4 cup chopped PLANTERS Pecans
- 1 Tbsp. butter or margarine, softened
- 1/4 tsp. ground cinnamon

Direction

- Heat oven to 350°F.
- Mash potatoes in large bowl. Add dressing, 1/4 cup sugar, ginger and zest; mix well.
- Spoon into 1-1/2-qt. casserole. Combine nuts, remaining sugar, butter and cinnamon; sprinkle over potato mixture.
- Bake 30 min. or until heated through.

Nutrition Information

- Calories: 200
- Sodium: 160 mg
- Cholesterol: 10 mg
- Fiber: 3 g
- Sugar: 22 g
- Saturated Fat: 1.5 g
- Total Fat: 7 g
- Total Carbohydrate: 32 g
- Protein: 2 g

93. Red Beans & Rice Soul Food Recipe

Serving: 0 | Prep: 10mins | Cook: 14hours30mins | Ready in: 14hours40mins

Ingredients

- 1 lb. dry red beans
- 12 slices OSCAR MAYER Bacon, cut into 1-inch-wide pieces
- 1 large onion, chopped
- 1 large green pepper, chopped
- 4 cloves garlic, minced
- 1 smoked ham hock (3/4 lb.)
- 3 cups fat-free reduced-sodium chicken broth
- 1/4 cup minced parsley, divided
- 1 bay leaf
- 2 tsp. Cajun seasoning
- 1 tsp. dried thyme leaves
- 1/4 tsp. ground red pepper (cayenne)
- 2 cups long-grain white rice (preferably converted), uncooked

Direction

- Rinse and pick through beans, discarding any misshapen beans or debris. Place beans in large bowl. Add enough water to cover beans by at least 2 inches. Let stand overnight.
- Drain beans, discarding soaking liquid; set beans aside. Cook bacon in Dutch oven or deep large skillet until crisp. Remove bacon from pan with slotted spoon, reserving 2 Tbsp. drippings in pan. Drain bacon on paper towels. Meanwhile, add onions, peppers and garlic to reserved drippings; cook and stir 5 min. or until crisp-tender.
- Return bacon to pan with beans, ham hock, broth, 2 Tbsp. parsley, bay leaf and seasonings. Bring to boil; simmer on low heat 2 to 2-1/2 hours or until beans are tender and liquid is thickened, stirring occasionally. Meanwhile, cook rice as directed on package during the last 30 min. of the bean cooking time.
- Remove ham hock and bay leaf; discard bay leaf. Shred meat from ham hock; discard bone and any fat. Stir meat into bean mixture. Serve over rice; top with remaining parsley.

Nutrition Information

- Calories: 510
- Total Fat: 9 g
- Saturated Fat: 3.5 g
- Protein: 30 g
- Sugar: 4 g
- Total Carbohydrate: 77 g
- Cholesterol: 40 mg
- Fiber: 16 g
- Sodium: 1050 mg

94. Simple Southern Style 'Unfried' Chicken

Serving: 8 | Prep: 15mins | Cook: 1hours15mins | Ready in: 1hours30mins

Ingredients

- 1 broiler-fryer chicken (4 lb.), cut up
- 1/2 cup KRAFT Lite Ranch Dressing
- 1 pkt. SHAKE 'N BAKE Extra Crispy Seasoned Coating Mix

Direction

- Remove skin from all chicken pieces except wings. Place chicken in large resealable plastic bag. Add dressing. Seal bag; turn to evenly coat chicken with dressing. Refrigerate 30 min. to marinate.
- Heat oven to 400°F. Place coating mix in pie plate or shallow dish. Dip chicken in coating mix, turning to evenly coat both sides of each piece. Place in single layer on baking sheet. Sprinkle with any remaining coating mix. Discard bag and marinade.
- Bake 40 to 45 min. or until chicken is done (165°F).

Nutrition Information

- Calories: 210
- Sugar: 0 g
- Sodium: 520 mg
- Fiber: 0 g
- Total Fat: 8 g
- Protein: 23 g
- Saturated Fat: 2 g
- Cholesterol: 70 mg
- Total Carbohydrate: 0 g

95. Slow Cooker Black Eyed Peas

Serving: 0 | Prep: 15mins | Cook: 6hours50mins | Ready in: 7hours5mins

Ingredients

- 1 lb. black-eyed peas, rinsed
- 4 carrots, peeled, chopped
- 1 large onion, chopped

- 4 slices OSCAR MAYER Bacon, chopped
- 2 cans (14-1/2 oz. each) fat-free reduced-sodium chicken broth
- 1 can (10 oz.) reduced-sodium diced tomatoes and green chiles, undrained
- 1 cup water
- 1 pkg. (7 oz.) OSCAR MAYER CARVING BOARD Slow Cooked Ham
- 1-1/2 tsp. ground cumin
- 1 bunch mustard greens, chopped
- 6 cups hot cooked long-grain white rice

Direction

- Place peas in large saucepan. Add enough water to cover by 3 inches. Bring to boil; simmer on medium-low heat 2 min. Remove from heat. Let stand, covered, 1 hour.
- Cook and stir carrots, onions and bacon in skillet on medium heat 8 min. or until onions are crisp-tender. Meanwhile, bring broth, tomatoes and water to boil in saucepan.
- Drain peas; place in slow cooker. Add cooked vegetables, broth mixture, ham and cumin; stir. Cover with lid; cook on LOW 5 to 6 hours (or on HIGH 2-1/2 to 3 hours).
- Stir in greens. Cook, covered, 30 min. or just until greens are tender. Serve with rice.

Nutrition Information

- Calories: 210
- Fiber: 4 g
- Protein: 10 g
- Total Fat: 2.5 g
- Cholesterol: 10 mg
- Saturated Fat: 0.5 g
- Total Carbohydrate: 0 g
- Sugar: 0 g
- Sodium: 370 mg

96. Sour Cream Beignets

Serving: 0 | Prep: 25mins | Cook: 2hours20mins | Ready in: 2hours45mins

Ingredients

- 1 pkg. (1/4 oz.) active dry yeast (not instant)
- 1/4 cup granulated sugar, divided
- 1/4 cup warm water (105°F to 115°F)
- 1 cup milk
- 1 cup BREAKSTONE'S or KNUDSEN Sour Cream
- 1 tsp. vanilla
- 1/2 tsp. baking soda
- 1/2 tsp. salt
- 4-1/2 to 5 cups flour, divided
- oil, for frying
- 3/4 cup powdered sugar

Direction

- Sprinkle yeast and 1 tsp. granulated sugar over warm water in large bowl; stir until dissolved. Let stand 5 min. Add remaining granulated sugar, milk, sour cream, vanilla, baking soda, salt and 4-1/2 cups flour; beat with mixer until well blended, stopping occasionally to scrape bottom and side of bowl. Stir in enough of the remaining flour to form soft dough.
- Place dough on lightly floured surface. Knead 10 min. or until smooth and elastic, gradually adding remaining flour if dough is too sticky. Place in well-greased bowl; turn dough so top is greased. Cover with plastic wrap. Let rise in warm place 1 hour or until doubled in volume.
- Punch down dough; place on sheet of lightly floured parchment paper. Roll into 12x9-inch rectangle. Use sharp knife or pizza wheel to cut dough into 48 (1-1/2-inch) squares; separate to allow 1 inch between squares. Cover with plastic wrap. Let rise in warm place 1 hour or until doubled in volume.
- Heat 1/2 inch oil in electric skillet to 350°F. Gently stretch each square of dough lengthwise into rectangle. Carefully add in batches to hot oil. (Do not crowd dough.) Cook

2 min. or until each beignet is golden brown on both sides, turning after 1 min. Place in single layer on paper towel-covered baking sheets. When all beignets are cooked, sprinkle with powdered sugar.

Nutrition Information

- Calories: 180
- Total Fat: 7 g
- Sugar: 7 g
- Total Carbohydrate: 26 g
- Fiber: 1 g
- Saturated Fat: 2 g
- Cholesterol: 10 mg
- Sodium: 85 mg
- Protein: 3 g

97. Southern Bacon Glazed Green Beans

Serving: 0 | Prep: 40mins | Cook: | Ready in: 40mins

Ingredients

- 6 slices OSCAR MAYER Bacon, cut into 1-inch-thick slices
- 1 small red onion, thinly sliced
- 2 lb. fresh green beans, trimmed
- 1 can (14.5 oz.) fat-free reduced-sodium chicken broth
- 1/4 cup packed brown sugar
- 2 Tbsp. HEINZ Apple Cider Vinegar
- 1/2 tsp. cracked black pepper

Direction

- Cook and stir bacon and onions in Dutch oven or small stockpot on medium heat until bacon is crisp. Remove bacon mixture from pan with slotted spoon; drain on paper towels. Discard all but 2 Tbsp. drippings from pan.
- Add beans and broth to reserved drippings; mix well. Bring to boil; cover. Simmer on medium-low heat 5 min. Add bacon mixture and all remaining ingredients; mix lightly. Return to boil; cook, uncovered, 7 to 9 min. or until beans are cooked to desired doneness, stirring occasionally.
- Use slotted spoon to transfer bean mixture to serving dish, reserving broth mixture in pan; cover beans to keep warm. Cook broth mixture 2 to 3 min. or until thickened to syrup-like consistency, stirring frequently. Pour over bean mixture.

Nutrition Information

- Calories: 130
- Total Carbohydrate: 15 g
- Fiber: 3 g
- Sugar: 11 g
- Protein: 5 g
- Sodium: 240 mg
- Total Fat: 6 g
- Saturated Fat: 2 g
- Cholesterol: 10 mg

98. Southern Shrimp And Grits

Serving: 4 | Prep: 25mins | Cook: | Ready in: 25mins

Ingredients

- 3/4 cup quick-cooking grits
- 2 slices OSCAR MAYER Bacon, cut into 1-inch pieces
- 3/4 lb. uncooked deveined peeled medium shrimp
- 4 green onions, thinly sliced
- 1 clove garlic, minced
- 2 Tbsp. chopped fresh parsley
- 1 Tbsp. lemon juice
- 1 cup KRAFT Shredded Cheddar Cheese

Direction

- Cook grits as directed on package.

- Meanwhile, cook and stir bacon in large skillet on medium-heat heat until crisp. Remove from skillet with slotted spoon; drain on paper towels. Add shrimp, onions and garlic to drippings in skillet; cook and stir 3 min. or until shrimp turn pink. Add bacon, parsley and lemon juice; mix well.
- Add cheese to grits; mix well. Serve topped with shrimp mixture.

Nutrition Information

- Calories: 370
- Fiber: 2 g
- Sodium: 1000 mg
- Total Fat: 18 g
- Saturated Fat: 9 g
- Sugar: 1 g
- Total Carbohydrate: 26 g
- Cholesterol: 195 mg
- Protein: 27 g

99. Southern Style Banana Pudding With Meringue

Serving: 0 | Prep: 30mins | Cook: 15mins | Ready in: 45mins

Ingredients

- 2 pkg. (3 oz. each) JELL-O Vanilla Flavor Cook & Serve Pudding
- 4-1/2 cups milk
- 3 eggs, separated
- 42 vanilla wafers (1/2 of 12-oz. pkg.)
- 2 large bananas, sliced
- dash cream of tartar
- 1/3 cup sugar

Direction

- Heat oven to 350°F.
- Beat pudding mixes and milk in medium saucepan with whisk until blended. Beat egg yolks in small bowl until blended. Gradually stir into milk mixture. Bring to full rolling boil on medium heat, stirring constantly. Remove from heat.
- Arrange layer of wafers on bottom and up side of 2-qt. baking dish. Top with layers of 1/3 of the pudding and half the banana slices. Repeat layers; cover with remaining pudding.
- Beat egg whites and cream of tartar in medium bowl with mixer on high speed until foamy. Gradually beat in sugar until stiff peaks form. Spread over pudding, sealing to edge of dish.
- Bake 15 min. or until meringue is browned. Cool.

Nutrition Information

- Calories: 250
- Saturated Fat: 2 g
- Sugar: 0 g
- Total Fat: 6 g
- Sodium: 240 mg
- Total Carbohydrate: 0 g
- Cholesterol: 55 mg
- Protein: 5 g
- Fiber: 0.5117 g

100. Southern Style Crab Cakes With Cool Lime Sauce

Serving: 9 | Prep: 25mins | Cook: | Ready in: 25mins

Ingredients

- zest and juice from 1 lime, divided
- 1 cup KRAFT Real Mayo Mayonnaise, divided
- 1 env. (0.7 oz.) GOOD SEASONS Italian Dressing Mix
- 2 Tbsp. GREY POUPON Country Dijon Mustard
- 2 cans (6 oz. each) crabmeat, drained, flaked
- 25 RITZ Crackers, finely crushed, divided
- 1 green onion, chopped

- 1/4 cup BREAKSTONE'S or KNUDSEN Sour Cream

Direction

- Mix half the lime juice, 1/2 cup mayo, dressing mix and mustard in medium bowl until blended. Add crabmeat, 1/2 cup cracker crumbs and onions; mix lightly.
- Shape into 18 (1/2-inch-thick) patties; coat with remaining cracker crumbs.
- Cook, in batches, in large nonstick skillet on medium heat 2 min. on each side or until heated through and golden brown on both sides. Meanwhile, mix sour cream, lime zest, and remaining mayo and lime juice until blended.
- Serve crab cakes with the lime sauce.

Nutrition Information

- Calories: 290
- Cholesterol: 50 mg
- Sodium: 770 mg
- Saturated Fat: 4.5 g
- Fiber: 0 g
- Total Carbohydrate: 0 g
- Sugar: 0 g
- Protein: 99 g
- Total Fat: 25 g

101. Spiked Peach Iced Tea

Serving: 0 | Prep: 10mins | Cook: | Ready in: 10mins

Ingredients

- 1 pkt. (makes 2 qt. drink) or 2 pkt. (makes 1 qt. drink each) CRYSTAL LIGHT Peach Flavor Iced Tea Mix*
- 4-1/2 cups water
- 1 cup orange juice
- 1/2 cup bourbon
- 6 orange slices

Direction

- Empty contents of drink mix packet into large plastic or glass pitcher. Add water, orange juice and bourbon; stir until drink mix is completely dissolved.
- Serve over ice cubes in tall glasses.
- Add orange slice to each glass.

Nutrition Information

- Calories: 90
- Total Fat: 0 g
- Cholesterol: 0 mg
- Sodium: 0 mg
- Total Carbohydrate: 6 g
- Sugar: 5 g
- Protein: 0 g
- Fiber: 0 g
- Saturated Fat: 0 g

Chapter 5: Hawaiian Recipes

***

102. 5 Minute Hot Hawaiian Dip

Serving: 0 | Prep: 5mins | Cook: | Ready in: 5mins

Ingredients

- 3/4 cup KRAFT Mayo with Olive Oil Reduced Fat Mayonnaise
- 1-1/2 cups KRAFT Shredded Sharp Cheddar Cheese, divided
- 1/4 cup BULL'S-EYE Brown Sugar & Hickory Barbecue Sauce
- 1 can (8 oz.) pineapple chunks in juice, drained

- 2 Tbsp. OSCAR MAYER Real Bacon Bits

Direction

- Mix mayo, 1 cup cheese and dressing; spread onto bottom of microwaveable pie plate. Microwave on HIGH 4 min.
- Top with pineapple, bacon and remaining cheese.
- Serve with your favorite crackers.

Nutrition Information

- Calories: 80
- Sodium: 170 mg
- Cholesterol: 10 mg
- Sugar: 2 g
- Total Carbohydrate: 4 g
- Total Fat: 6 g
- Saturated Fat: 2 g
- Fiber: 0 g
- Protein: 2 g

103. BBQ Hawaiian Naan Pizza

Serving: 0 | Prep: 20mins | Cook: | Ready in: 20mins

Ingredients

- 6 oz. fresh pineapple, cut into 2 (3/4-inch-thick) rings
- 3 oz. ham steak
- 1 pkg. (9 oz.) naan breads (2 breads)
- 1/4 cup BULL'S-EYE or KRAFT Original Barbecue Sauce
- 3/4 cup KRAFT Shredded Colby & Monterey Jack Cheeses

Direction

- Heat grill to medium heat.
- Grill pineapple and ham 8 min., turning after 4 min. Transfer to cutting board; chop into 1/2-inch pieces. Reduce grill to medium-low heat.
- Brush naan with barbecue sauce to within 1/2 inch of edges; top with pineapple, ham and cheese.
- Grill 2 to 3 min. or until bottoms of pizzas are lightly browned and cheese is melted.

Nutrition Information

- Calories: 350
- Total Carbohydrate: 44 g
- Saturated Fat: 5 g
- Cholesterol: 30 mg
- Fiber: 2 g
- Total Fat: 12 g
- Sodium: 860 mg
- Protein: 15 g
- Sugar: 11 g

104. Blue Hawaiian Recipe

Serving: 0 | Prep: 15mins | Cook: | Ready in: 15mins

Ingredients

- 2 Tbsp. BAKER'S ANGEL FLAKE Coconut, toasted
- 2 small fresh pineapple wedges
- 1/2 cup pineapple juice
- 3 Tbsp. blue curaçao liqueur
- 3 Tbsp. rum
- 3 Tbsp. cream of coconut
- 2 cups crushed ice

Direction

- Place coconut on small plate.
- Cut slit in each pineapple wedge from point end to center of wedge. Dip, 1 at a time, into coconut, turning to evenly coat both sides of each wedge.
- Blend all remaining ingredients except ice in blender until blended. Add ice; blend on high speed until smooth.

- Pour into 2 glasses. Place pineapple wedge on rim of each glass.

Nutrition Information

- Calories: 340
- Fiber: 1 g
- Protein: 1 g
- Saturated Fat: 6 g
- Cholesterol: 0 mg
- Sodium: 40 mg
- Total Carbohydrate: 45 g
- Total Fat: 6 g
- Sugar: 37 g

105. Canadian Bacon Hawaiian Pizza Recipe

Serving: 2 | Prep: 5mins | Cook: 10mins | Ready in: 15mins

Ingredients

- 1 Italian pizza crust (8 inch)
- 1/4 cup CLASSICO Traditional Pizza Sauce
- 1/2 cup KRAFT 2% Milk Shredded Mozzarella Cheese
- 2 slices Canadian bacon, quartered
- 1/4 cup well-drained canned pineapple tidbits

Direction

- Heat oven to 450°F. Place crust on baking sheet; spread with sauce.
- Top with remaining ingredients.
- Bake 8 to 10 min. or until cheese is melted.

Nutrition Information

- Calories: 390
- Protein: 20 g
- Fiber: 1 g
- Saturated Fat: 4.5 g
- Sodium: 1040 mg
- Cholesterol: 25 mg
- Total Carbohydrate: 53 g
- Sugar: 4 g
- Total Fat: 11 g

106. Easy No Bake Hawaiian Marshmallow Pie

Serving: 8 | Prep: 15mins | Cook: 3hours30mins | Ready in: 3hours45mins

Ingredients

- 24 JET-PUFFED Miniature Marshmallows
- 2 cans (8 oz. each) crushed pineapple, drained with 1/2 cup liquid reserved
- 2 cups thawed COOL WHIP Whipped Topping
- 1 ready-to-use graham cracker crumb crust (6 oz.)

Direction

- Microwave marshmallows and reserved pineapple liquid in large microwaveable bowl on HIGH 2 to 3 min. or until marshmallows are completely melted and mixture is well blended, stirring after each minute.
- Refrigerate 30 min. or until slightly thickened; stir until blended. Gently stir in pineapple and COOL WHIP; pour into crust.
- Refrigerate 3 hours or until firm.

Nutrition Information

- Calories: 200
- Fiber: 1 g
- Total Carbohydrate: 0 g
- Protein: 1 g
- Saturated Fat: 6 g
- Total Fat: 9 g
- Sugar: 0 g
- Cholesterol: 0 mg
- Sodium: 95 mg

107. Grilled Hawaiian Quesadillas

Serving: 4 | Prep: 20mins | Cook: 10mins | Ready in: 30mins

Ingredients

- 2 cans (8 oz. each) pineapple rings in juice, drained
- 1/4 cup KRAFT Mayo with Olive Oil Reduced Fat Mayonnaise
- 1 Tbsp. chopped canned chipotle peppers in adobo sauce
- 4 flour tortillas (8 inch)
- 16 slices OSCAR MAYER Deli Fresh Smoked Ham
- 1 cup KRAFT Shredded Monterey Jack Cheese

Direction

- Heat grill to medium-low heat.
- Grill pineapple rings 2 min. on each side or until heated through; cut in half.
- Mix mayo and peppers until blended; spread onto tortillas.
- Top with ham, cheese and pineapple; fold in half.
- Grill 3 min. on each side or until golden brown on both sides.
- Cut into wedges to serve.

Nutrition Information

- Calories: 400
- Protein: 18 g
- Fiber: 5 g
- Saturated Fat: 8 g
- Sodium: 1110 mg
- Total Carbohydrate: 36 g
- Sugar: 10 g
- Cholesterol: 50 mg
- Total Fat: 20 g

108. Ham And Cheese Sandwich Strata

Serving: 6 | Prep: 15mins | Cook: 50mins | Ready in: 1hours5mins

Ingredients

- 6 slices Hawaiian sliced bread
- 6 tsp. GREY POUPON Savory Honey Mustard
- 6 KRAFT Big Slice Sharp Cheddar Cheese Slices
- 12 slices OSCAR MAYER Natural Applewood Smoked Ham
- 2 eggs
- 1/2 cup milk
- 1/4 cup maple-flavored or pancake syrup

Direction

- Heat oven to 350°F.
- Spread bread with mustard. Place 2 bread slices, mustard sides up, in single layer in 9x5-inch loaf pan sprayed with cooking spray; press to completely cover bottom of pan. Cover with 3 cheese slices, 6 ham slices and 2 of the remaining bread slices, mustard sides down. Top with remaining cheese and ham slices; cover with remaining bread slices, mustard sides down.
- Whisk remaining ingredients until blended; pour over strata. Let stand 5 min.
- Bake 45 to 50 min. or until knife inserted in center comes out clean and top is golden brown. Let stand 15 min. Run knife around edges of pan to loosen strata; invert onto platter. Remove pan. Cut strata into 6 slices to serve.

Nutrition Information

- Calories: 40
- Protein: 0.671 g

- Saturated Fat: 0 g
- Sugar: 0 g
- Cholesterol: 0 mg
- Sodium: 20 mg
- Total Carbohydrate: 0 g
- Total Fat: 0 g
- Fiber: 0 g

109. Hawaiian BBQ Glazed Pork Chops

Serving: 4 | Prep: 20mins | Cook: |Ready in: 20mins

Ingredients

- 3/4 cup BULL'S-EYE Original Barbecue Sauce
- 1 can (8 oz.) crushed pineapple in juice in juice, undrained
- 1/4 tsp. each nutmeg, ground red pepper and dry mustard
- 2 Tbsp. chopped fresh basil
- 4 bone-in pork chops (1-1/2 lb.), 1/2 inch thick

Direction

- Heat grill to medium heat.
- Mix all ingredients except chops until blended. Reserve 1/2 cup sauce for serving with the cooked chops.
- Grill chops 5 min. on each side. Brush with some of the remaining sauce; grill 3 to 4 min. or until chops are done (145°F), turning occasionally and brushing with remaining sauce.
- Remove chops from grill. Let stand 3 min. before serving with the reserved sauce.

Nutrition Information

- Calories: 280
- Sodium: 640 mg
- Protein: 24 g
- Total Fat: 6 g
- Saturated Fat: 2 g

- Cholesterol: 60 mg
- Sugar: 0 g
- Fiber: 1 g
- Total Carbohydrate: 0 g

110. Hawaiian Chicken Recipe

Serving: 4 | Prep: 30mins | Cook: 30mins |Ready in: 1hours

Ingredients

- 2 tsp. cornstarch
- 1/2 cup pineapple juice
- 1/2 cup MR. YOSHIDA'S Original Gourmet Sauce
- 1 Tbsp. olive oil
- 1 tsp. crushed red pepper
- 4 small boneless skinless chicken breasts (1 lb.)

Direction

- Mix cornstarch and pineapple juice until blended. Add all remaining ingredients except chicken; mix well.
- Pour half the pineapple juice mixture over chicken in shallow dish; turn to evenly coat both sides of each breast with pineapple juice mixture. Refrigerate 30 min. to marinate.
- Heat grill to medium heat. Remove chicken from marinade; discard marinade. Grill chicken 6 to 8 min. on each side or until done (165°F). Meanwhile, bring remaining pineapple juice mixture to boil in saucepan on medium heat, stirring constantly; simmer on medium-low heat 5 min. or until thickened, stirring frequently.
- Serve chicken topped with pineapple sauce.

Nutrition Information

- Calories: 240
- Fiber: 0 g

- Total Carbohydrate: 0 g
- Sodium: 760 mg
- Protein: 26 g
- Cholesterol: 65 mg
- Saturated Fat: 1 g
- Sugar: 0 g
- Total Fat: 5 g

111. Hawaiian Cilantro Lime Chicken Kabobs

Serving: 8 | Prep: 30mins | Cook: 2hours10mins | Ready in: 2hours40mins

Ingredients

- 2 lb. boneless skinless chicken breasts, cut into 1-1/2-inch pieces
- 1 cup KRAFT Zesty Lime Vinaigrette Dressing, divided
- 1/2 tsp. pepper
- 2 each green and red bell peppers, cut into 1-1/2-inch pieces
- 1/2 sweet onion, cut into wedges
- 2 cups fresh pineapple chunks
- 2 limes, cut into wedges
- 2 Tbsp. chopped fresh cilantro

Direction

1. Add chicken pieces to a large zipper top plastic bag. Add 1/2 cup of the dressing and pepper to the bag. Seal the bag and use hands to massage the dressing into the chicken. Place in the refrigerator and let sit for 2 hours.
2. Place the fruit and vegetables into a new large zipper top plastic bag; add 1/4 cup of the dressing. Seal the bag and use hands to massage the dressing into the vegetables and fruit. Place in refrigerator and let sit for 2 hours.
3. Soak eight 12-inch wooden skewers in water 1 hour before using them so they do not burn when on the grill.
4. When you are ready to grill, pull the chicken, vegetables and fruit out of the refrigerator. Remove chicken from marinade; discard marinade. Remove vegetables and fruit from marinade; discard marinade. Thread chicken, pineapple and vegetables alternately onto skewers ending each skewer with a wedge of lime saving the marinade for grilling.
5. Heat the grill to medium-high heat. Grill 8 to 10 min. or until chicken is done, turning occasionally. Brush the kabobs with remaining dressing towards the end of grilling.
6. Serve the kabobs with fresh cilantro sprinkled over top and the grilled lime wedges for extra flavor.

Nutrition Information

- Calories: 200
- Fiber: 3 g
- Protein: 19 g
- Sugar: 0 g
- Sodium: 300 mg
- Total Carbohydrate: 0 g
- Total Fat: 7 g
- Saturated Fat: 1 g
- Cholesterol: 55 mg

112. Hawaiian Club Dogs

Serving: 0 | Prep: 10mins | Cook: 10mins | Ready in: 20mins

Ingredients

- 6 OSCAR MAYER Wieners
- 6 slices OSCAR MAYER Bacon
- 1-1/4 cups finely chopped fresh pineapple
- 2 green onions, sliced
- 6 hot dog buns
- 1/3 cup KRAFT Real Mayo Mayonnaise

Direction

- Cook wieners and bacon as directed on packages.
- Combine pineapple and onions.
- Spread buns with mayo; fill with wieners, bacon and pineapple mixture.

Nutrition Information

- Calories: 420
- Cholesterol: 55 mg
- Protein: 13 g
- Saturated Fat: 8 g
- Sugar: 0 g
- Total Fat: 30 g
- Total Carbohydrate: 0 g
- Sodium: 880 mg
- Fiber: 2 g

113. Hawaiian Coffee For Two

Serving: 0 | Prep: 10mins | Cook: | Ready in: 10mins

Ingredients

- 1-1/3 cups warm milk
- 1-1/3 cups BAKER'S ANGEL FLAKE Coconut
- 1/4 cup MAXWELL HOUSE Coffee, any variety
- 1-1/4 cups water

Direction

- Blend milk and coconut in blender on high speed 40 sec.; pour through fine-mesh strainer into empty pot of coffee maker. While still holding strainer over coffee pot, press coconut with back of spoon to remove as much liquid as possible; discard strained solids.
- Place coffee in filter in brew basket of coffee maker. Add water to coffee maker; brew. When brewing is complete, stir until blended.

Nutrition Information

- Calories: 150
- Total Fat: 10 g
- Saturated Fat: 8 g
- Fiber: 1 g
- Sugar: 9 g
- Cholesterol: 15 mg
- Sodium: 80 mg
- Protein: 6 g
- Total Carbohydrate: 10 g

114. Hawaiian Cookie Balls

Serving: 32 | Prep: 30mins | Cook: 50mins | Ready in: 1hours20mins

Ingredients

- 1 can (8 oz.) crushed pineapple in juice, undrained
- 1 pkg. (3.4 oz.) JELL-O Vanilla Flavor Instant Pudding
- 40 square shortbread cookies, finely crushed (about 3 cups)
- 1-1/2 pkg. (4 oz. each) BAKER'S White Chocolate (6 oz.), broken into pieces, melted
- 3/4 cup BAKER'S ANGEL FLAKE Coconut

Direction

- Combine pineapple and dry pudding mix in medium bowl. Immediately stir in cookie crumbs. Refrigerate 30 min.
- Shape into 32 (1-inch) balls. Roll 16 balls in coconut; place on waxed paper-covered rimmed baking sheet. Dip remaining balls in melted chocolate; add to baking sheet.
- Refrigerate 20 min. or until firm.

Nutrition Information

- Calories: 100
- Protein: 0.7841 g
- Saturated Fat: 2.5 g
- Cholesterol: 0 mg

- Sodium: 100 mg
- Total Fat: 4.5 g
- Sugar: 0 g
- Total Carbohydrate: 0 g
- Fiber: 0 g

115. Hawaiian Cookies

Serving: 0 | Prep: 20mins | Cook: 2hours10mins | Ready in: 2hours30mins

Ingredients

- 1/2 cup butter, softened
- 4 oz. (1/2 of 8-oz. pkg.) PHILADELPHIA Cream Cheese, softened
- 1 tsp. vanilla
- 3/4 cup powdered sugar
- 2 cups flour
- 3/4 cup finely chopped toasted PLANTERS Macadamias
- 1 pkg. (4 oz.) BAKER'S White Chocolate

Direction

- Beat butter, cream cheese and vanilla in large bowl with mixer until creamy. Add sugar; beat until light and fluffy. Gradually add flour, mixing well after each addition. Add nuts; mix well.
- Shape dough into ball; flatten into disc. Wrap tightly in plastic wrap.
- Refrigerate 2 hours or until firm.
- Roll out dough on lightly floured surface to 1/4-inch thickness. Cut into shapes using 2-inch pineapple-shaped or round cookie cutter. Place, 2 inches apart, onto baking sheets. Refrigerate 30 min.
- Heat oven to 350°F. Bake cutouts 8 to 10 min. or until edges are lightly browned. Cool 1 min. Remove to wire racks; cool completely.

Nutrition Information

- Calories: 160
- Cholesterol: 15 mg
- Saturated Fat: 4.5 g
- Sodium: 55 mg
- Total Carbohydrate: 0 g
- Total Fat: 10 g
- Fiber: 0.5491 g
- Sugar: 0 g
- Protein: 2 g

116. Hawaiian Flatbread Appetizer

Serving: 0 | Prep: 10mins | Cook: 20mins | Ready in: 30mins

Ingredients

- 1 whole wheat tortilla (10 inch)
- 1/4 cup KRAFT Pineapple Spread
- 1-1/2 cups baby spinach leaves
- 8 slices OSCAR MAYER Deli Fresh Smoked Ham, chopped
- 2 Tbsp. shaved red onions

Direction

- Heat oven to 400°F.
- Place tortilla on baking sheet. Bake 5 min.; cool 5 min.
- Spread with pineapple spread; top with remaining ingredients.
- Bake 10 min.

Nutrition Information

- Calories: 50
- Sodium: 180 mg
- Protein: 3 g
- Cholesterol: 10 mg
- Sugar: 0 g
- Total Carbohydrate: 0 g
- Total Fat: 2 g
- Saturated Fat: 1 g

- Fiber: 0 g

117. Hawaiian Jalapeño Bacon Pizza

Serving: 6 | Prep: 10mins | Cook: 12mins | Ready in: 22mins

Ingredients

- 1 ready-to-use baked pizza crust (12 inch)
- 1/4 cup CLASSICO Traditional Pizza Sauce
- 1/2 cup KRAFT Shredded Cheddar Cheese
- 1/2 cup KRAFT Shredded Mozzarella Cheese
- 1/3 cup OSCAR MAYER Real Bacon Recipe Pieces
- 1/2 cup drained canned crushed pineapple in juice
- 1/3 cup drained pickled jalapeño nacho slices

Direction

- Heat oven to 425°F.
- Spread pizza crust with sauce; sprinkle with half each of the cheddar and mozzarella.
- Top with bacon, pineapple, jalapeños and remaining cheeses.
- Bake 12 min. or until cheeses are melted.

Nutrition Information

- Calories: 250
- Fiber: 1 g
- Total Fat: 10 g
- Protein: 11 g
- Sodium: 700 mg
- Total Carbohydrate: 0 g
- Saturated Fat: 4.5 g
- Cholesterol: 20 mg
- Sugar: 0 g

118. Hawaiian Pineapple Spread

Serving: 0 | Prep: 10mins | Cook: 25mins | Ready in: 35mins

Ingredients

- 2 jars (5 oz. each) KRAFT Pineapple Spread
- 1 pkg. (8 oz.) PHILADELPHIA Cream Cheese, softened
- 6 slices OSCAR MAYER Baked Cooked Ham, finely chopped
- 1 cup KRAFT Shredded Low-Moisture Part-Skim Mozzarella Cheese
- 4 green onions, sliced

Direction

- Heat oven to 350°F.
- Mix ingredients until blended.
- Spread onto bottom of 9-inch pie plate sprayed with cooking spray.
- Bake 20 to 25 min. or until heated through.

Nutrition Information

- Calories: 70
- Protein: 3 g
- Cholesterol: 20 mg
- Fiber: 0 g
- Saturated Fat: 3 g
- Total Carbohydrate: 2 g
- Sugar: 2 g
- Total Fat: 5 g
- Sodium: 150 mg

119. Hawaiian Sausage Sliders

Serving: 8 | Prep: 20mins | Cook: | Ready in: 20mins

Ingredients

- 1 pkg. (12 oz.) OSCAR MAYER Natural Uncured Beef Sausage

- 4 fresh pineapple rings (1/4 inch thick)
- 8 Hawaiian sweet rolls, split
- 3 Tbsp. KRAFT Light Mayo Reduced Fat Mayonnaise
- 1/4 tsp. ground red pepper (cayenne)
- 1/8 tsp. onion powder
- 1/8 tsp. garlic powder
- 8 small lettuce leaves

Direction

- Heat grill to medium-high heat.
- Cut sausage into 8 pieces, then partially cut each piece lengthwise in half.
- Place sausage, cut sides down, on grill grate; grill 3 to 4 min. on each side or until heated through. Remove from grill.
- Grill pineapple 1 to 2 min. on each side or until heated through. Remove from grill; cut in half.
- Place rolls, cut sides down, on grill grate; grill 1 to 2 min. or until lightly toasted.
- Mix mayo and seasonings until blended; spread onto cut sides of rolls. Fill with sausage, pineapple and lettuce.

Nutrition Information

- Calories: 270
- Sodium: 570 mg
- Saturated Fat: 4.5 g
- Total Fat: 12 g
- Protein: 10 g
- Fiber: 1 g
- Sugar: 0 g
- Cholesterol: 30 mg
- Total Carbohydrate: 0 g

120. Hawaiian Tamales

Serving: 0 | Prep: 20mins | Cook: 1hours | Ready in: 1hours20mins

Ingredients

- 52 corn husks
- 52 Tamale Dough
- 1 to 2 Tbsp. KOOL-AID Cherry Flavor Sugar-Sweetened Drink Mix
- 3 cups chopped fresh or canned pineapple, drained
- 1 cup firmly packed brown sugar

Direction

- Soak corn husks in hot water 30 minutes or let stand overnight in room-temperature water. Prepare Tamale Dough recipe, adding the drink mix to the dough with the masa harina.
- Assemble tamales by spreading 2 Tbsp. of the masa mixture (tamale dough) into a 3x2-inch rectangle down the center of each corn husk, leaving about 2 inches bare at the top of the husk. Spoon 1 Tbsp. of the pineapple and 1 tsp. of the brown sugar down the center of the masa mixture; fold over the sides of the husk and both ends to completely enclose the filling.
- Stand tamales in a steamer basket in large pot filled 1/4 full with water. (Make sure tamales are not touching the water.) Bring water to boil; cover. Steam 1 hour or until tamales pull away from the corn husks, adding more water to the pot when necessary. Remove tamales from steamer basket; cool slightly. Top with thawed COOL WHIP Whipped Topping just before serving, if desired.

Nutrition Information

- Calories: 220
- Fiber: 2 g
- Sugar: 10 g
- Total Fat: 13 g
- Cholesterol: 10 mg
- Sodium: 310 mg
- Protein: 2 g
- Total Carbohydrate: 25 g
- Saturated Fat: 5 g

121. Luau Meatballs

Serving: 6 | Prep: 20mins | Cook: |Ready in: 20mins

Ingredients

- 1 pkg. (16 oz.) frozen fully cooked meatballs
- 1 cup MR. YOSHIDA'S Hawaiian Sweet & Sour Sauce
- 1 can (8 oz.) pineapple chunks in juice, drained

Direction

- Cook meatballs and sweet-and-sour sauce in medium saucepan on medium heat 15 min or until heated through, stirring frequently.
- Add pineapple; mix well. Cook and stir 5 min. or until heated through.

Nutrition Information

- Calories: 300
- Total Fat: 20 g
- Total Carbohydrate: 0 g
- Saturated Fat: 8 g
- Sodium: 970 mg
- Fiber: 1 g
- Cholesterol: 35 mg
- Sugar: 0 g
- Protein: 12 g

122. Luau Sandwich With Hawaiian Bread

Serving: 0 | Prep: 5mins | Cook: |Ready in: 5mins

Ingredients

- 1 slice Hawaiian sliced bread, cut in half
- 1 Tbsp. KRAFT Real Mayo Mayonnaise
- 1 KRAFT Big Slice Swiss Cheese Slice
- 5 slices OSCAR MAYER Deli Fresh Honey Ham
- 2 tsp. chopped fresh cilantro
- 2 drained canned pineapple slices
- 2 thin red onion slices

Direction

- Spread bread with mayonnaise; fill with remaining ingredients.

Nutrition Information

- Calories: 360
- Total Fat: 20 g
- Saturated Fat: 7 g
- Total Carbohydrate: 29 g
- Cholesterol: 50 mg
- Fiber: 1 g
- Protein: 17 g
- Sodium: 840 mg
- Sugar: 13 g

123. Mini Crab Sandwich Recipe

Serving: 0 | Prep: 20mins | Cook: |Ready in: 20mins

Ingredients

- 1 pkg. (12 oz.) Hawaiian savory butter rolls (12 rolls)
- 2 cans (6 oz. each) lump crabmeat, drained, flaked
- 1/2 cup chopped red peppers
- 1 stalk celery, chopped
- 1/4 cup KRAFT Mayo Homestyle Real Mayonnaise
- 1 Tbsp. GREY POUPON Dijon Mustard
- 1 Tbsp. seafood seasoning
- 1 Tbsp. lemon zest
- 4 romaine lettuce leaves, quartered

Direction

- Heat oven to 325°F.
- Cut rolls horizontally in half; place, cut sides up, on baking sheet.

- Bake 8 min. Meanwhile, combine all remaining ingredients except lettuce.
- Fill rolls with lettuce and crabmeat mixture just before serving.

Nutrition Information

- Calories: 330
- Total Fat: 13 g
- Total Carbohydrate: 32 g
- Protein: 19 g
- Fiber: 0.7879 g
- Cholesterol: 75 mg
- Sodium: 520 mg
- Saturated Fat: 4 g
- Sugar: 8 g

124. Quick Hawaiian Pork "Kabob" Foil Packages

Serving: 4 | Prep: 15mins | Cook: 15mins | Ready in: 30mins

Ingredients

- 2 cups instant white rice, uncooked
- 1-1/3 cups water
- 1 pork tenderloin (1 lb.), cut into bite-size pieces
- 2 red peppers, chopped
- 1 can (8 oz.) pineapple tidbits, drained
- 1 small onion, sliced
- 1/2 cup KRAFT Zesty Italian Dressing

Direction

- Heat grill to medium heat.
- Combine rice and water; spoon onto centers of 4 large sheets heavy-duty foil. Top evenly with remaining ingredients.
- Fold foil to make 4 packets.
- Grill 15 min. or until meat is done and rice is tender. Cut slits in foil to release steam before opening packets.

Nutrition Information

- Calories: 400
- Cholesterol: 60 mg
- Total Fat: 9 g
- Saturated Fat: 2 g
- Fiber: 3 g
- Protein: 26 g
- Sugar: 0 g
- Total Carbohydrate: 0 g
- Sodium: 360 mg

125. Weeknight Hawaiian Pizza

Serving: 8 | Prep: 25mins | Cook: | Ready in: 25mins

Ingredients

- 1 can (13.8 oz.) refrigerated pizza crust
- 1 cup CLASSICO Traditional Pizza Sauce
- 18 slices OSCAR MAYER Deli Fresh Smoked Ham, chopped
- 1 can (8 oz.) pineapple tidbits, drained
- 1-1/2 cups KRAFT Shredded Low-Moisture Part-Skim Mozzarella Cheese
- 1/2 cup sliced red onions
- 1/2 tsp. dried Italian seasoning

Direction

- Heat oven to 425°F.
- Unroll pizza crust onto 12-inch round pizza pan sprayed with cooking spray; press to edge of pan. Bake 8 min.
- Spread crust with pizza sauce. Top with remaining ingredients.
- Bake 10 min. or until edge of crust is golden brown and cheese is melted.

Nutrition Information

- Calories: 220

- Total Carbohydrate: 0 g
- Total Fat: 6 g
- Cholesterol: 20 mg
- Sugar: 0 g
- Saturated Fat: 3 g
- Sodium: 880 mg
- Protein: 13 g
- Fiber: 1 g

Chapter 6: Mediterranean Recipes

***

126.   5 Layer Greek Dip

Serving: 0 | Prep: 10mins | Cook: | Ready in: 10mins

Ingredients

- 1 pkg. (7 oz.) ATHENOS Original Hummus
- 1 pkg. (4 oz.) ATHENOS Traditional Feta Cheese, crumbled
- 1 medium tomato, chopped
- 1/4 cup chopped cucumbers
- 2 Tbsp. sliced black olives
- 2 bags (9 oz.) ATHENOS Pita Chips Original

Direction

- Spread hummus onto bottom of 9-inch pie plate.
- Cover with layers of remaining ingredients.
- Serve with chips.

Nutrition Information

- Calories: 180
- Sugar: 0 g
- Saturated Fat: 1 g
- Cholesterol: 5 mg
- Protein: 6 g
- Total Fat: 8 g
- Fiber: 3 g
- Sodium: 480 mg
- Total Carbohydrate: 0 g

127.   Cedar Planked Mediterranean Chicken

Serving: 0 | Prep: 15mins | Cook: 5hours15mins | Ready in: 5hours30mins

Ingredients

- 2 untreated cedar planks (14x7x1 inch each)
- 1 cup KRAFT Greek Vinaigrette Dressing
- 1/2 cup finely chopped fresh parsley, divided
- Grated peel and juice of 1 lemon
- 4 large bone-in chicken breasts with skin (4 lb.)
- 2 Tbsp. oil
- 1/4 cup chopped pitted Kalamata olives

Direction

- Immerse planks in water, placing a weight on top of each plank to keep it submerged. Soak at least 4 hours or overnight.
- Meanwhile, mix dressing, 1/4 cup of the parsley, the lemon zest and juice until well blended. Remove 1/4 cup of the dressing mixture; set aside for later use. Pour remaining dressing mixture into large resealable plastic bag; add chicken. Seal bag; turn over several times to evenly coat chicken with the dressing mixture. Refrigerate at least 2 hours.
- Preheat grill to medium heat. Remove planks from water; brush tops with oil. Remove chicken from marinade; discard bag and marinade. Place 2 chicken breasts on each plank. Place on grate of grill; cover with lid.
- Grill 1 to 1-1/4 hours or until chicken is cooked through (165ºF). Meanwhile, mix

reserved dressing mixture, remaining 1/4 cup parsley and the olives. Remove chicken from grill; discard planks. Remove bones from chicken; cut each breast in half. Serve topped with the parsley mixture.

Nutrition Information

- Calories: 280
- Cholesterol: 85 mg
- Total Carbohydrate: 0 g
- Sodium: 270 mg
- Saturated Fat: 3.5 g
- Sugar: 0 g
- Protein: 29 g
- Total Fat: 17 g
- Fiber: 0 g

128. Cheese Topped Grilled Tomatoes

Serving: 4 | Prep: 10mins | Cook: 12mins | Ready in: 22mins

Ingredients

- 4 plum tomatoes, cut lengthwise in half
- 1/4 cup KRAFT Lite Zesty Italian Dressing
- 1/2 cup KRAFT Shredded Low-Moisture Part-Skim Mozzarella Cheese
- 2 Tbsp. KRAFT Grated Parmesan Cheese
- 1 Tbsp. chopped fresh herbs (basil, chives and/or parsley)

Direction

- Heat grill to medium-high heat.
- Place tomatoes, cut-sides up, in 8-inch square foil pan sprayed with cooking spray. Drizzle with dressing; top with cheeses. Place pan on grill grate.
- Grill 10 to 12 min. or until mozzarella is melted and tomatoes are heated through.
- Sprinkle with herbs.

Nutrition Information

- Calories: 80
- Saturated Fat: 2.5 g
- Sugar: 3 g
- Fiber: 1 g
- Total Fat: 4.5 g
- Cholesterol: 10 mg
- Sodium: 320 mg
- Total Carbohydrate: 5 g
- Protein: 6 g

129. Creamy Mediterranean Dip

Serving: 0 | Prep: 10mins | Cook: | Ready in: 10mins

Ingredients

- 1-1/2 cups BREAKSTONE'S or KNUDSEN Cottage Cheese
- 1 pkg. (10 oz.) frozen chopped spinach, thawed, drained
- 1/3 cup KRAFT Italian Roasted Red Pepper Dressing

Direction

- Mix ingredients until blended.
- Serve with cut-up fresh vegetables.

Nutrition Information

- Calories: 25
- Sugar: 0 g
- Protein: 2 g
- Saturated Fat: 0.5 g
- Fiber: 0 g
- Sodium: 115 mg
- Total Fat: 1 g
- Total Carbohydrate: 0 g
- Cholesterol: 5 mg

130. Feta Cheese Mediterranean Salad

Serving: 0 | Prep: 15mins | Cook: | Ready in: 15mins

Ingredients

- 4 cups tightly packed torn mixed salad greens
- 1 cup chopped plum tomatoes
- 1 cup coarsely chopped Kalamata olives
- 1 avocado, chopped
- 1 pkg. (4 oz.) ATHENOS Traditional Crumbled Feta Cheese
- 3/4 cup rinsed canned chickpeas (garbanzo beans)
- 1/2 cup slivered red onions
- 1/2 cup KRAFT Balsamic Vinaigrette Dressing

Direction

- Combine all ingredients except dressing in large bowl.
- Add dressing just before serving; mix lightly.

Nutrition Information

- Calories: 370
- Total Carbohydrate: 0 g
- Protein: 12 g
- Cholesterol: 20 mg
- Sodium: 1120 mg
- Saturated Fat: 5 g
- Fiber: 9 g
- Total Fat: 27 g
- Sugar: 0 g

131. Grilled Chicken Pitas

Serving: 4 | Prep: 15mins | Cook: 30mins | Ready in: 45mins

Ingredients

- 1/2 cup A.1. Smoky Black Pepper Sauce
- 2 Tbsp. brown sugar
- 2 Tbsp. lemon juice
- 1/2 tsp. ground black pepper
- 1 lb. boneless skinless chicken breasts, cut into 1/4-inch-thick slices
- 4 whole wheat pita breads, cut in half
- 2 cups loosely packed baby spinach leaves
- 1 cucumber, thinly sliced
- 1 cup chopped tomatoes
- 1/2 cup ATHENOS Crumbled Feta Cheese with Mediterranean Herbs

Direction

- Mix first 4 ingredients until blended. Reserve half the A.1. mixture; pour remaining over chicken in shallow dish. Stir to evenly coat chicken. Refrigerate 30 min. to marinate.
- Heat grill to medium heat. Remove chicken from marinade; discard marinade. Grill chicken 5 to 7 min. or until done, turning after 4 min. and adding pitas to the grill for the last 2 min. to grill 1 min. on each side.
- Fill pita halves with spinach, cucumbers, chicken and tomatoes. Drizzle with reserved A.1. mixture. Top with cheese.

Nutrition Information

- Calories: 440
- Sodium: 1160 mg
- Sugar: 0 g
- Total Fat: 8 g
- Total Carbohydrate: 0 g
- Fiber: 7 g
- Cholesterol: 80 mg
- Saturated Fat: 3.5 g
- Protein: 36 g

132. Mediterranean Bean Salad Recipe

Serving: 0 | Prep: 10mins | Cook: | Ready in: 10mins

Ingredients

- 1 can (15 oz.) white kidney beans, rinsed
- 1 can (14 oz.) artichoke hearts, drained, quartered
- 1 cup halved cherry tomatoes
- 1/2 cup KRAFT Finely Shredded Italian* Five Cheese Blend
- 1/2 cup pitted black olives
- 1/4 cup chopped red onions
- 2 Tbsp. chopped parsley
- 1/3 cup KRAFT Sun Dried Tomato Vinaigrette Dressing

Direction

- Combine ingredients.

Nutrition Information

- Calories: 140
- Total Carbohydrate: 0 g
- Sugar: 0 g
- Fiber: 6 g
- Cholesterol: 5 mg
- Sodium: 640 mg
- Total Fat: 5 g
- Saturated Fat: 1.5 g
- Protein: 7 g

133. Mediterranean Chicken

Serving: 0 | Prep: 5mins | Cook: 15mins | Ready in: 20mins

Ingredients

- 2 cups instant brown rice, uncooked
- 4 small boneless skinless chicken breasts (1 lb.)
- 1 small onion, chopped
- 1 tsp. dried oregano leaves
- 1 can (14-1/2 oz.) Italian-style diced tomatoes, drained
- 1/4 cup KRAFT Sun Dried Tomato Vinaigrette Dressing
- 2 tsp. minced garlic
- 1/4 cup sliced pimento-stuffed green olives

Direction

- Cook rice as directed on package.
- Meanwhile, heat large nonstick skillet sprayed with cooking spray on medium heat. Add chicken, onions and oregano; cook 6 min. or until chicken is lightly browned on both sides and onions are crisp-tender, turning chicken after 3 min. Add tomatoes, dressing and garlic; stir gently. Cook 4 to 6 min. or until chicken is done (165ºF), turning chicken after 3 min. Stir in olives.
- Spoon rice onto platter; top with chicken and sauce.

Nutrition Information

- Calories: 360
- Cholesterol: 65 mg
- Protein: 29 g
- Sodium: 720 mg
- Saturated Fat: 1.5 g
- Sugar: 0 g
- Total Fat: 8 g
- Total Carbohydrate: 0 g
- Fiber: 3 g

134. Mediterranean Chicken Recipe

Serving: 0 | Prep: 5mins | Cook: 20mins | Ready in: 25mins

Ingredients

- 4 small boneless skinless chicken breasts (1 lb.)

- 1 can (14-1/2 oz.) Italian-style diced tomatoes, undrained
- 1/2 cup black olives, chopped
- 1 Tbsp. lemon zest
- 1 cup KRAFT Finely Shredded Italian* Five Cheese Blend
- 3 cups hot cooked rotini pasta

Direction

- Heat large nonstick skillet on medium-high heat. Add chicken; cover. Cook 5 to 7 min. on each side or until done (165°F). Remove chicken from skillet.
- Add tomatoes, olives and lemon zest to skillet. Cook 4 min. or until hot, stirring frequently.
- Return chicken to skillet; cook 1 min. or until hot. Top with cheese. Serve over pasta.

Nutrition Information

- Calories: 410
- Fiber: 3 g
- Total Carbohydrate: 0 g
- Sugar: 0 g
- Total Fat: 11 g
- Saturated Fat: 5 g
- Cholesterol: 85 mg
- Protein: 38 g
- Sodium: 970 mg

135. Mediterranean Chicken And Mushroom Skillet

Serving: 4 | Prep: 35mins | Cook: | Ready in: 35mins

Ingredients

- 1 Tbsp. olive oil
- 4 small boneless skinless chicken breasts (1 lb.)
- 1 lb. sliced fresh mushrooms
- 1 onion, finely chopped
- 1/2 cup chicken broth
- 1 clove garlic, minced

- 1/2 tsp. dried thyme leaves
- 1/2 cup ATHENOS Traditional Crumbled Feta Cheese
- 1 Tbsp. chopped fresh parsley

Direction

- Heat oil in large nonstick skillet on medium-high heat. Add chicken; cook 6 to 8 min. on each side or until done (165°F). Remove chicken from skillet, reserving drippings in skillet; cover chicken to keep warm.
- Add mushrooms and onions to drippings; cook 10 min., stirring occasionally. Add broth, garlic and thyme; stir. Cook 5 min.; stir in cheese.
- Top chicken with mushroom mixture and parsley.

Nutrition Information

- Calories: 250
- Fiber: 2 g
- Sugar: 0 g
- Total Carbohydrate: 0 g
- Saturated Fat: 3.5 g
- Total Fat: 10 g
- Sodium: 350 mg
- Protein: 32 g
- Cholesterol: 80 mg

136. Mediterranean Chicken And Sausage Recipe

Serving: 12 | Prep: 15mins | Cook: 45mins | Ready in: 1hours

Ingredients

- 1 lb. sweet Italian sausage
- 1/2 cup KRAFT Greek Vinaigrette Dressing, divided
- 1 roasting chicken, cut up (3 lb.)
- 1/2 lb. medium mushrooms, halved

- 1 can (14-1/2 oz.) fat-free reduced-sodium chicken broth
- 2 Tbsp. cornstarch
- 1/4 cup water
- 6 cups hot cooked instant white rice

Direction

- Pierce sausage with fork. Cook in large skillet on medium-high heat 15 to 20 min. or until browned. Remove from skillet. Cut into pieces; set aside.
- Add 1/4 cup of the dressing and chicken to skillet; cook 10 min. or until chicken is browned on both sides. Stir in sausage, mushrooms, broth and remaining dressing.
- Dissolve cornstarch in water; add to skillet. Bring to boil. Reduce heat to low; cover. Simmer 15 min. or until chicken is cooked through. Serve over rice.

Nutrition Information

- Calories: 350
- Protein: 17 g
- Cholesterol: 55 mg
- Sugar: 0 g
- Total Carbohydrate: 0 g
- Sodium: 360 mg
- Total Fat: 16 g
- Fiber: 0.8557 g
- Saturated Fat: 4.5 g

137. Mediterranean Couscous Salad

Serving: 0 | Prep: 15mins | Cook: 1hours | Ready in: 1hours15mins

Ingredients

- 1 pkg. (10 oz.) couscous
- 1/2 cup KRAFT Italian Dressing
- 3 Tbsp. GREY POUPON Dijon Mustard
- 1/2 tsp. grated lemon zest
- 1 pkg. (4 oz.) ATHENOS Traditional Feta Cheese, crumbled
- 1/3 cup chopped drained roasted red peppers
- 1/2 cup chopped pitted black olives

Direction

- Prepare couscous as directed on package; cool slightly. Beat dressing, mustard and lemon zest with wire whisk until well blended.
- Combine cheese, peppers and olives in large bowl; stir in couscous. Add dressing mixture; toss to coat well. Cover.
- Refrigerate at least 1 hour before serving.

Nutrition Information

- Calories: 320
- Sugar: 0 g
- Saturated Fat: 4 g
- Total Fat: 13 g
- Cholesterol: 15 mg
- Fiber: 3 g
- Sodium: 700 mg
- Total Carbohydrate: 0 g
- Protein: 10 g

138. Mediterranean Halibut With Mushroom Rice Pilaf

Serving: 0 | Prep: 25mins | Cook: | Ready in: 25mins

Ingredients

- 1/4 cup KRAFT Greek Vinaigrette Dressing, divided
- 1 lb. halibut fillets
- 2 cups sliced fresh mushrooms
- 1-3/4 cups water
- 2 cups instant brown rice, uncooked
- 1 cup frozen peas, thawed

Direction

- Heat oven to 450°F.
- Drizzle 2 Tbsp. dressing over fish in shallow baking dish.
- Bake 15 min. or until fish flakes easily with fork. Meanwhile, cook mushrooms in remaining dressing in medium skillet 3 to 4 min. or until mushrooms are tender, stirring occasionally. Add water; bring to boil. Stir in rice and peas; cover. Simmer 5 min. Remove from heat; let stand 5 min.
- Spoon rice mixture onto serving plates; top with fish.

Nutrition Information

- Calories: 350
- Total Carbohydrate: 0 g
- Sodium: 270 mg
- Fiber: 4 g
- Sugar: 0 g
- Saturated Fat: 1.5 g
- Cholesterol: 55 mg
- Protein: 27 g
- Total Fat: 9 g

139. Mediterranean Marinated Vegetable Salad

Serving: 0 | Prep: 15mins | Cook: 1hours | Ready in: 1hours15mins

Ingredients

- 2 large tomatoes, cut into wedges
- 1 each green and yellow pepper, coarsely chopped
- 1 zucchini, cut lengthwise in half, sliced
- 1/4 cup red onion wedges
- 1/2 cup KRAFT Zesty Italian Dressing
- 2 Tbsp. chopped fresh basil
- 2 cloves garlic, minced
- 1 cup KRAFT Natural Three Cheese Crumbles

Direction

- Combine vegetables in large bowl.
- Mix dressing, basil and garlic. Add to vegetable mixture; toss to coat.
- Add cheese; mix lightly. Refrigerate 1 hour.

Nutrition Information

- Calories: 110
- Total Fat: 8 g
- Saturated Fat: 3 g
- Sodium: 250 mg
- Sugar: 0 g
- Total Carbohydrate: 0 g
- Cholesterol: 15 mg
- Fiber: 1 g
- Protein: 4 g

140. Mediterranean Mozza Chicken

Serving: 0 | Prep: 10mins | Cook: 18mins | Ready in: 28mins

Ingredients

- 4 small boneless skinless chicken breasts (1 lb.)
- 1 red onion, cut lengthwise in half, then sliced crosswise
- 1 zucchini, chopped
- 1/4 cup KRAFT Tuscan House Italian Dressing
- 1/2 cup halved grape tomatoes
- 1/2 cup pitted black olives
- 1 cup KRAFT 2% Milk Shredded Mozzarella Cheese

Direction

- Heat large nonstick skillet on medium-high heat. Add chicken; cover skillet with lid. Cook 5 to 7 min. on each side or until chicken is done (165°F), adding onions and zucchini after 5 min.

- Add dressing, tomatoes and olives; cover. Cook on medium-low heat 2 min. or until heated through; stir.
- Top with cheese; cook, covered, 2 min. or until melted.

Nutrition Information

- Calories: 300
- Sodium: 540 mg
- Total Carbohydrate: 0 g
- Fiber: 2 g
- Total Fat: 15 g
- Sugar: 0 g
- Protein: 33 g
- Cholesterol: 80 mg
- Saturated Fat: 4.5 g

141. Mediterranean Pork Medallions

Serving: 0 | Prep: 10mins | Cook: 18mins | Ready in: 28mins

Ingredients

- 1/2 cup KRAFT Sun Dried Tomato Vinaigrette Dressing made with Extra Virgin Olive Oil, divided
- 1 cup frozen cut green beans
- 1 can (14 oz.) fat-free reduced-sodium chicken broth
- 2 cups instant white rice, uncooked
- 1 pork tenderloin (1 lb.), cut crosswise into 8 slices
- 1 tsp. dried rosemary leaves, crushed
- 1 cup chopped plum tomatoes (about 2 medium)
- 2 Tbsp. KRAFT Grated Parmesan Cheese

Direction

- Heat 1/4 cup of the dressing in medium saucepan on medium heat. Add beans; cook 1 min. Stir in broth. Bring to boil. Reduce heat to medium-low; simmer 2 to 3 min. or until beans are crisp-tender. Add rice. Return to boil; cover. Remove from heat; let stand 5 min. or until liquid is absorbed.
- Meanwhile, pound meat with meat mallet to 1/2-inch thickness; sprinkle with rosemary. Heat remaining 1/4 cup dressing in large nonstick skillet. Add meat; cook 4 min. on each side or until cooked through.
- Place two of the meat medallions on each of four individual serving plates; top with the reserved liquid from skillet. Add tomatoes and cheese to rice mixture; stir. Serve with the meat.

Nutrition Information

- Calories: 410
- Sodium: 700 mg
- Total Carbohydrate: 0 g
- Fiber: 3 g
- Protein: 33 g
- Total Fat: 10 g
- Sugar: 0 g
- Saturated Fat: 3 g
- Cholesterol: 70 mg

142. Mediterranean Quinoa Salad Recipe

Serving: 0 | Prep: 20mins | Cook: 30mins | Ready in: 50mins

Ingredients

- 2 cups fat-free reduced-sodium chicken broth
- 1 cup quinoa, uncooked
- 1 cup cherry tomatoes, halved
- 1 small English cucumber, chopped
- 1 small red onion, cut lengthwise in half, then crosswise into thin slices
- 1/2 cup KRAFT Greek Vinaigrette Dressing, divided

- 10 cups tightly packed torn romaine lettuce
- 1/2 cup ATHENOS Traditional Crumbled Feta Cheese

Direction

- Bring broth and quinoa to boil in saucepan on high heat; simmer on medium-low heat 15 min. or until liquid is absorbed. Cool.
- Combine tomatoes, cucumbers and onions in medium bowl. Add 1/4 cup dressing; mix lightly.
- Cover platter with lettuce; top with quinoa, vegetable mixture and cheese. Drizzle with remaining dressing.

Nutrition Information

- Calories: 150
- Fiber: 4 g
- Sugar: 0 g
- Sodium: 390 mg
- Cholesterol: 5 mg
- Protein: 6 g
- Total Fat: 6 g
- Total Carbohydrate: 0 g
- Saturated Fat: 1.5 g

143. Mediterranean Salmon For Two

Serving: 2 | Prep: 25mins | Cook: | Ready in: 25mins

Ingredients

- 2 skinless salmon fillets (1/2 lb.)
- 1/4 cup KRAFT Lite Balsamic Vinaigrette Dressing, divided
- 2 cloves garlic, minced
- 1 pkg. (6 oz.) baby spinach leaves
- 4 tsp. KRAFT Grated Parmesan Cheese, divided

Direction

- Heat oven to 400°F.
- Place fish in shallow baking dish; drizzle with 3 Tbsp. dressing. Bake 10 to 12 min. or until fish flakes easily with fork.
- Meanwhile, heat remaining dressing in large skillet on medium heat. Add garlic; cook and stir 1 min. Stir in spinach; cover. Cook 2 min.; uncover. Cook 30 sec. or just until spinach is wilted, turning frequently with tongs.
- Place spinach on 2 serving plates; sprinkle evenly with 2 tsp. cheese. Top with fish and dressing from baking dish. Sprinkle with remaining cheese.

Nutrition Information

- Calories: 260
- Total Carbohydrate: 0 g
- Sodium: 410 mg
- Cholesterol: 60 mg
- Sugar: 0 g
- Protein: 24 g
- Total Fat: 14 g
- Saturated Fat: 3.5 g
- Fiber: 2 g

144. Mediterranean Herbed Scallops Recipe

Serving: 0 | Prep: 10mins | Cook: 10mins | Ready in: 20mins

Ingredients

- 1 lb. sea scallops, well dried
- 1/4 tsp. pepper
- 2 Tbsp. butter
- 2 plum tomatoes, chopped
- 1 clove garlic, minced
- 1/2 cup dry white wine
- 1/2 cup fat-free reduced-sodium chicken broth
- 10 pitted Kalamata olives, sliced
- 2 Tbsp. chopped fresh chives, divided
- 1 Tbsp. chopped fresh mint

- 1 Tbsp. fresh lime juice
- 1/3 cup ATHENOS Traditional Crumbled Feta Cheese
- 4 cups hot cooked fusilli pasta

Direction

- Sprinkle scallops with pepper. Melt butter in large nonstick skillet on medium-high heat. Add single layer of scallops; cook 2 to 3 min. on each side or just until firm and browned on both sides. Remove from heat; cover to keep warm.
- Add tomatoes and garlic to skillet; cook and stir on medium heat 1 min. Stir in wine, broth and olives; simmer 2 min. or until liquid is reduced by half.
- Stir in 1 Tbsp. each chives, mint and lime juice. Add scallops; stir. Simmer on low heat 1 min. or until heated through. Add pasta; toss to coat. Transfer to bowl; top with cheese and remaining chives.

Nutrition Information

- Calories: 420
- Sodium: 590 mg
- Sugar: 3 g
- Total Fat: 12 g
- Cholesterol: 70 mg
- Protein: 28 g
- Fiber: 3 g
- Saturated Fat: 5 g
- Total Carbohydrate: 45 g

145. Mixed Greens With Mediterranean Vinaigrette

Serving: 6 | Prep: 10mins | Cook: | Ready in: 10mins

Ingredients

- 3 Tbsp. HEINZ Red Wine Vinegar
- 2 cloves garlic, minced
- 1 tsp. GREY POUPON Dijon Mustard
- 1 tsp. sugar
- 1/4 tsp. pepper
- 1/4 cup extra virgin olive oil
- 1 pkg. (10 oz.) torn mixed salad greens
- 1 pkg. (4 oz.) ATHENOS Traditional Crumbled Feta Cheese

Direction

- Blend first 5 ingredients in blender until well blended. Add oil; blend 15 sec.
- Place greens in large bowl. Add dressing; toss to coat.
- Top with cheese.

Nutrition Information

- Calories: 140
- Total Carbohydrate: 4 g
- Protein: 5 g
- Sugar: 0.7086 g
- Cholesterol: 15 mg
- Total Fat: 13 g
- Sodium: 300 mg
- Fiber: 1 g
- Saturated Fat: 4 g

146. Olive & Cheese Appetizers

Serving: 0 | Prep: 15mins | Cook: 2mins | Ready in: 17mins

Ingredients

- 1/3 cup KRAFT Real Mayo Mayonnaise
- 1 tsp. garlic powder
- 1 pkg. (8 oz.) KRAFT Finely Shredded Mozzarella Cheese
- 2 medium tomatoes, seeded, chopped (about 1 cup)
- 1 can (4-1/4 oz.) chopped pitted black olives, drained

- 2 loaves French bread (about 24 inches each)

Direction

- Preheat broiler to high. Mix mayo and garlic powder in small bowl. Stir in cheese, tomato and olives.
- Cut each bread loaf diagonally into 24 slices; place on baking sheet. Spread evenly with cheese mixture.
- Broil, 4 to 6 inches from heat, 2 min. or until cheese is melted. Serve warm.

Nutrition Information

- Calories: 80
- Sugar: 0 g
- Protein: 3 g
- Cholesterol: 5 mg
- Total Fat: 3 g
- Sodium: 180 mg
- Saturated Fat: 1 g
- Fiber: 1 g
- Total Carbohydrate: 11 g

147. Shrimp Kabobs With Olive And Tomato Relish

Serving: 0 | Prep: 15mins | Cook: 8mins | Ready in: 23mins

Ingredients

- 1/4 cup KRAFT Balsamic Vinaigrette Dressing, divided
- 1 lb. uncooked large shrimp, peeled, deveined
- 1 small red onion, cut into 1-inch chunks
- 1 lemon, cut into 8 wedges
- 1/4 cup chopped black olives
- 1/4 cup chopped tomatoes

Direction

- Heat grill to medium-high heat. Reserve 2 Tbsp. dressing. Thread shrimp and onions alternately onto 4 skewers; thread lemon wedges onto ends. Brush with remaining dressing.
- Grill 6 to 8 min. or until shrimp turn pink, turning occasionally. Meanwhile, mix reserved dressing with olives and tomatoes.
- Serve kabobs topped with olive mixture.

Nutrition Information

- Calories: 160
- Sugar: 0 g
- Sodium: 440 mg
- Saturated Fat: 0.5 g
- Total Carbohydrate: 0 g
- Protein: 24 g
- Fiber: 2 g
- Total Fat: 4.5 g
- Cholesterol: 220 mg

148. Simple 'Stuffed Artichoke' Appetizer

Serving: 12 | Prep: 15mins | Cook: 30mins | Ready in: 45mins

Ingredients

- 2 cans (14 oz. each) medium artichoke hearts, drained, halved lengthwise
- 1/4 cup KRAFT Grated Parmesan Cheese
- 1/4 cup Italian-seasoned panko bread crumbs
- 3 cloves garlic, minced
- 2 Tbsp. olive oil, divided

Direction

- Heat oven to 425°F.
- Arrange artichokes in concentric circles on bottom of 9-inch pie plate sprayed with cooking spray.
- Combine cheese, bread crumbs, garlic and 1 Tbsp. oil; sprinkle over artichokes. Drizzle with remaining oil.

- Bake 30 min. or until heated through.

Nutrition Information

- Calories: 70
- Cholesterol: 5 mg
- Sugar: 0 g
- Sodium: 190 mg
- Saturated Fat: 1 g
- Protein: 3 g
- Fiber: 1 g
- Total Carbohydrate: 0 g
- Total Fat: 3 g

149. Spicy Feta Dip With Roasted Red Peppers

Serving: 0 | Prep: 10mins | Cook: | Ready in: 10mins

Ingredients

- 1 pkg. (3.5 oz.) ATHENOS Crumbled Reduced Fat Feta Cheese, divided
- 1 jar (7 oz.) roasted red peppers, drained, patted dry
- 1/4 cup plain nonfat Greek-style yogurt
- 1/8 tsp. crushed red pepper

Direction

- Reserve 1 Tbsp. cheese. Process remaining cheese with remaining ingredients in food processor until smooth.
- Serve topped with reserved cheese.

Nutrition Information

- Calories: 30
- Cholesterol: 5 mg
- Protein: 3 g
- Saturated Fat: 1 g
- Total Carbohydrate: 0 g
- Sugar: 0 g
- Total Fat: 1.5 g

- Sodium: 210 mg
- Fiber: 0 g

150. Zesty Feta And Vegetable Rotini Salad

Serving: 0 | Prep: 30mins | Cook: 1hours | Ready in: 1hours30mins

Ingredients

- 3 cups tri-colored rotini pasta, cooked, cooled
- 1 cup ATHENOS Traditional Crumbled Feta Cheese
- 1 cup halved cherry tomatoes
- 1 cup chopped cucumbers
- 1/2 cup sliced black olives
- 1/2 cup KRAFT Zesty Italian Dressing
- 1/4 cup finely chopped red onions

Direction

- Combine ingredients.
- Refrigerate 1 hour.

Nutrition Information

- Calories: 210
- Sugar: 0 g
- Protein: 8 g
- Fiber: 2 g
- Saturated Fat: 2.5 g
- Cholesterol: 10 mg
- Total Carbohydrate: 0 g
- Sodium: 410 mg
- Total Fat: 8 g

Index

A
Almond 3,5,14,26,27

Apple 4,18,47,48,55,60

Artichoke 4,79

Asparagus 3,6

Avocado 46

B
Bacon 3,4,7,12,16,49,51,52,54,55,58,59,62,65

Baking 4,11,39,45,46

Banana 4,45,56

Beans 4,52,55

Beef 3,6,20,21,29,31,50,65

Biscuits 4,45,46

Bread 4,67

Burger 4,50

Butter 3,4,33,35,39,46

C
Cabbage 3,23

Cake 4,56

Caramel 41,46

Cashew 24,36,38,43

Catfish 4,51

Cheddar 49,55,57,60,65

Cheese 4,11,12,17,18,22,26,35,36,37,43,45,48,49,51,55,57,58,59,60,64,65,67,68,69,70,71,72,73,74,75,76,77,78,79,80

Cherry 66

Chestnut 3,16

Chicken 3,4,5,7,8,9,14,16,18,19,23,24,25,27,30,33,34,35,36,37,38,40,41,42,44,47,50,53,61,62,69,71,72,73,75

Chickpea 3,34

Chips 11,69

Chocolate 3,11,12,37,63,64

Chutney 3,35,43

Cider 18,47,55

Coconut 3,26,28,36,37,58,63

Coffee 3,4,17,63

Couscous 4,74

Crab 4,56,67

Crackers 10,49,56

Cream 3,4,11,12,17,18,22,26,34,35,36,37,43,45,54,57,64,65,70

Crumble 71,73,75,77,78,80

Cucumber 3,10,42

Curry 3,18,36,37,38,42,43,44

D
Dal 3,40

E
Egg 3,12

F
Fat 5,6,7,8,9,10,11,12,13,14,15,16,17,18,19,20,21,22,23,24,25,26,27,28,29,30,31,32,33,34,35,36,37,38,39,40,41,42,43,44,45,46,47,48,49,50,51,52,53,54,55,56,57,58,59,60,61,62,63,64,65,66,67,68,69,70,71,72,73,74,75,76,77,78,79,80

Feta 4,69,71,73,74,77,78,80

Fish 3,44

Flatbread 4,64

French bread 79

Fruit 41

G
Garlic 13,20

Gin 3,29,30

H

Halibut 4,74

Ham 4,29,50,54,60,64,65,67,68

Herbs 71

Honey 60,67

Hummus 69

K

Ketchup 6,8,12

L

Lemon 3,25

Lime 4,32,36,38,56,62

M

Macadamia 64

Macaroni 4,48,49

Mango 3,43

Marshmallow 4,59

Mayonnaise 46,50,56,57,60,62,66,67,78

Meat 3,4,21,67

Meringue 4,56

Milk 59,75

Mozzarella 49,59,65,68,70,75,78

Mushroom 4,73,74

Mustard 47,56,60,67,74,78

N

Noodles 3,9,15,18,21,23,27

Nut 5,6,7,8,9,10,11,12,13,14,15,16,17,18,19,20,21,22,23,24,25,26,27,28,29,30,31,32,33,34,35,36,37,38,39,40,41,42,43,44,45,46,47,48,49,50,51,52,53,54,55,56,57,58,59,60,61,62,63,64,65,66,67,68,69,70,71,72,73,74,75,76,77,78,79,80

O

Oil 15,33,46,50,57,60,76

Olive 4,15,33,50,57,60,76,78,79

Onion 26

Orange 3,24,29

P

Pancakes 3,11

Parmesan 51,70,76,77,79

Pasta 32

Peach 4,51,57

Peanuts 5,7,8,9,10,19,21,23,29

Peas 3,4,16,53

Pecan 45,46,52

Pepper 4,15,32,70,71,80

Pie 4,24,38,59,65,74

Pineapple 3,4,28,64,65

Pizza 4,58,59,65,68

Pork 3,4,5,6,13,15,25,47,61,68,76

Potato 4,52

Praline 4,52

Q

Quinoa 4,76

R

Rice 3,4,7,12,18,29,36,43,52,74

S

Salad 3,4,10,13,14,19,23,27,48,71,72,74,75,76,80

Salmon 3,4,10,77

Salt 8

Sausage 4,65,73

Savory 60

Scallop 4,77

Seasoning 9,15,23,27

Shortbread 3,11

Soup 3,30,32

Steak 3,13,15

Stew 3,34

Sugar
3,5,6,7,8,9,10,11,12,13,14,15,16,17,18,19,20,21,22,23,24,2
5,26,27,28,29,30,31,32,33,34,35,36,37,38,39,40,41,42,43,4
4,45,46,47,48,49,50,51,52,53,54,55,56,57,58,59,60,61,62,6
3,64,65,66,67,68,69,70,71,72,73,74,75,76,77,78,79,80

T

Taco 4,47

Tapioca 3,28,51

Tea 4,57

Teriyaki 3,8,9,15,16

Tilapia 3,4,17,46

Tofu 3,31

Tomato 3,4,12,33,34,44,70,72,76,79

Truffle 3,12

Turkey 50

V

Vegetables 13,14

Vegetarian 3,40

Vinegar 13,18,47,55,78

W

Walnut 13,14

Wine 78

Worcestershire sauce 9

Z

Zest 4,16,22,25,30,32,36,38,50,62,68,70,75,80

Conclusion

Thank you again for downloading this book!

I hope you enjoyed reading about my book!

If you enjoyed this book, please take the time to share your thoughts and post a review on Amazon. It'd be greatly appreciated!

Write me an honest review about the book – I truly value your opinion and thoughts and I will incorporate them into my next book, which is already underway.

Thank you!

If you have any questions, **feel free to contact at:** *author@shrimpcookbook.com*

Penny Cook

shrimpcookbook.com

Printed in Great Britain
by Amazon